EB5 2.0
THE INSTITUTIONALIZATION OF EB5

EB5 2.0

THE INSTITUTIONALIZATION OF EB-5

Changes in Legislation, China, and the Role of the Broker-Dealer

KEVIN WRIGHT AND
MICHAEL FITZPATRICK

LIONCREST
PUBLISHING

EB5 2.0 | THE INSTITUTIONALIZATION OF EB5

Changes in Legislation, China, and the Role of the Broker-Dealer

ISBN   978-1-5445-1169-6 *Hardcover*

      978-1-5445-1168-9 *Paperback*

      978-1-5445-1167-2 *Ebook*

CONTENTS

INTRODUCTION

The Employment-Based Fifth Preference (EB-5) program bears many similarities to immigrant investor programs in other countries. Administered by US Citizenship and Immigration Services (USCIS), EB-5 offers a three-way value proposition to investors, developers, and the US economy. Investors, their spouses, and unmarried children under the age of twenty-one obtain a pathway to more quickly immigrate to the US by making a qualifying investment, while developers gain access to capital that is inexpensive, relative to market-rate mezzanine loans or preferred equity. The US economy and taxpayers benefit because the program attracts foreign capital that creates at least ten jobs per investor, enhances the tax base where the EB-5 qualifying project is located, and is cost-neutral to the federal budget, as the program is self-sustaining with program fees.

The EB-5 program first launched in 1990, but it largely flew under the radar for many years, until the advent of the Regional Center Pilot Program in 1992 and the recession of 2008. In the wake of the Great Recession, traditional capital markets dried up, and real estate developers turned increasingly to the EB-5 program as a source to fill funding gaps for their projects. However, its rise in popularity without significant regulatory oversight produced an environment ripe for fraud and aggressive sales practices. Recent political debates have called aspects of the program into question, leaving the primary stakeholders—regional centers, developers, and investors—unsure of what the future holds.

THE STATE OF CHINA

Until recently, China supplied as much as 85 percent of all EB-5 investors. However, China has become a victim of its own success. Regulations limit EB-5 visas to 10,000 a year, which are initially earmarked at 7 percent for each eligible country (though, as we'll discuss later, this may change). At the end of the US government's fiscal year, all remaining visas are made available to any country that exceeded its initial allotment of 700. Chinese investors have scooped those up, but once global demand exceeded 10,000 EB-5 visas, "retrogression," or a backlog of investors, began with China. Vietnam hit retrogression in April 2018, as did India in October 2018, but China's problem has been growing for years.

The current backlog of Chinese investors is estimated at 100,000 visas, which represents a waiting line of fifteen years (as of April 2018), assuming the rest of the world only claims 2,000 EB-5 visas annually. Complicating the long wait are USCIS rules that ensure children of EB-5 investors will "age out" while they wait for a conditional green card. Clearly, the long wait has dampened demand from China, slowed the flow of EB-5 capital into the US, and triggered numerous unanticipated consequences. Further complicating investment from China are state-imposed restrictions on taking capital out of the country.

THE NEW WORLD

With demand for EB-5 in China down 80 to 90 percent from its peak, developers and regional centers have turned to other countries that have historically shown interest in EB-5. But these countries lack the infrastructure of China, which has a mature migration-agent industry that has educated the largest market in the world and, until retrogression, efficiently sourced enough EB-5 capital to meet the demand of US developers. In addition to adapting to cultural differences, which impacts the structure of the EB-5 capital, developers and regional centers are forging new ground to access investors, while maintaining compliance with securities laws and the USA PATRIOT Act and sorting through challenges to adequately document the investor's source of funds (SOF).

Long reliant on the Regulation S exemption from securities registration to market overseas, developers and regional centers increasingly work with registered broker-dealers to market EB-5 under Regulation D within the US to persons present on a temporary visa, such as H-1B or a student visa. Working with a broker-dealer to market within the US also brings the comfort of robust compliance with US securities laws.

AN UNCERTAIN FUTURE

EB-5 legislation contains both a permanent portion and a portion subject to periodic renewal. The permanent portion of the law prescribes the creation of ten direct jobs per $1,000,000 investment, or $500,000 if the investment is located within a Targeted Employment Area (TEA). A direct job is one that can be observed or noted on a payroll report. A TEA is a geographic area that contains the project and is marked by unemployment 1.5 times the national average. Under the current law, the state where a TEA is located prescribes the certification process, and states have widely different protocols and requirements for certifying TEAs.

The EB-5 Regional Center Pilot Program requires periodic legislative renewal. Regional centers are entities certified by USCIS to aggregate passive EB-5 investment capital. The primary benefit of using a regional center is the ability to count indirect and induced jobs, in addition to direct jobs, to meet the job creation requirement of ten new US jobs per investor. Indirect and induced jobs are calculated by an economist, using software such as IMPLAN or RIMS II, based on the capital used to build the project and the revenue and expenses of operating the project or business.

Congress and industry stakeholders have been unable to create long-term legislation for the stability for the program, forcing the regional center program to depend on short-term extensions, a situation that creates uncertainty in the marketplace. Several failed attempts at a long-term solution have identified the components necessary for a solution, including technical changes to fulfill the original intent of the program and integrity measures, but Congress and industry lobbyists have failed to agree on the tactics to achieve these objectives. As a result, legislative efforts have stalled, with no end in sight.

Even so, legislative intent is in the eye of the beholder, so while job creation seems like the clear end goal, the road to achieving it can take many turns. Aspects of the program under consideration to shape the legislative intent include the redefining of TEAs, the differential in the capital investment inside and outside of TEAs, and the use of priority visas.

The reputational damage brought about by several fraud cases in the industry, magnified in the press due to the program's link to the politically charged issue of immigration, further complicates EB-5 legislation. Relative to other capital markets, EB-5 is small (under 1 percent of all green cards issued annually) and until recently had largely gone unnoticed by regulators. Passage of any long-term renewal of the regional center program should include robust integrity and compliance measures.

Integrity measures drafted in proposed legislation, and draft regulations that USCIS may impose in the absence of new legislation, require developers and regional centers to certify compliance with securities laws, compliance with the offer, and disclosure of all material facts (including the names of those compensated for sourcing investors). Unless the regional center and project sponsor control and manage the network sourcing investors, certifying compliance poses risks that could expose the sponsor to a right of rescission.

Working with a Financial Industry Regulatory Authority (FINRA) broker-dealer mitigates the risk of noncompliance, and it may enhance the marketability of the project by conferring credibility to investors that comes through investing with an independent party that is regulated by the SEC.

Finally, all prior versions of draft legislation and the proposed regulations increase the regulatory burden for regional centers and projects. Regional centers that have operated as "rent-a-centers" with a lean back office will be faced with investing in overhead or outsourcing their compliance needs, which include enhanced project due diligence, stringent know-your-customer (KYC), and anti-money-laundering (AML) requirements, periodic site visits and audits by USCIS, and increased annual fees to establish the Employment Creation Visa Integrity Fund to cover the costs for USCIS to administer the higher compliance standards.

This book assumes the reader has a grasp of the basic concepts of the EB-5 industry and the concerns of the primary stakeholders. Part 1 of the book examines current market conditions in China, how the market is reacting to take EB-5 to the rest of the world, and the resulting impact on the primary EB-5 stakeholders. Part 2 of the book examines failed attempts for long-term EB-5 legislation and what will likely be included as part of any long-term renewal of the program, along with the resulting impact on the primary stakeholders.

PART ONE

THE MARKET TODAY

CHAPTER ONE

THE STATE OF CHINA

A decade ago, relatively few people promoted or used EB-5 visas in China. No one anticipated widespread interest in the country, so the number of investors from China resembled the number of investors from other countries, with fewer than 2,000 of 10,000 visas claimed each year.

THE RISE OF EB-5 IN CHINA

With the worldwide economic crisis beginning in 2008, developers in the US sought alternative sources of capital in order to bring projects to completion, and the EB-5 program began to attract greater attention. Promoters saw tremendous opportunity in China, so they began to aggressively promote EB-5 in that country. Within a few years, the number of Chinese investor applications exploded, and a backlog quickly developed.

USCIS estimates that, as of the second quarter of the 2017 fiscal year, there were 22,152 pending I-526 petitions.[1] This number fails to take into account family members who also need visas, bringing the total number of people in line to well over 100,000. With only 10,000 visas available per country, this backlog appears insurmountable without legislative intervention.

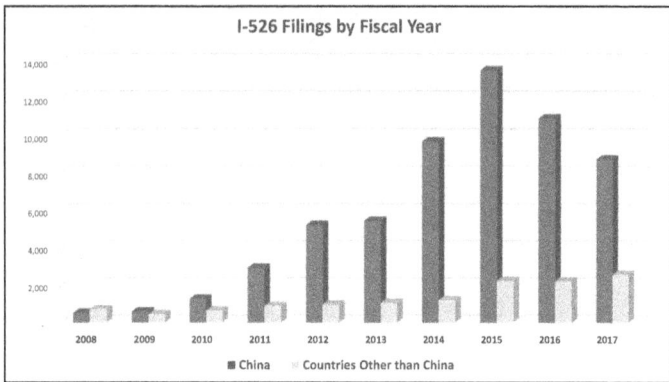

I-526 Filings by Fiscal Year

Source: USCIS presentation to AILA/IIUSA Conference Chicago October 30, 2018

How can we possibly begin to address the problem?

PREDICTABLY UNPREDICTABLE

The section of EB-5 legislation related to regional centers requires periodic renewal. An EB-5 regional center is an organization serving a specific geographical region composed of economically linked areas, such as counties, metropolitan statistical areas, combined statistical areas,

---

1   Bernard Wolfsdorf, Esq., *White Paper: Solutions to the EB-5 Visa Waiting Line* (American Immigration Lawyers Association EB-5 Committee, 2017), 3, Washington DC

or states. These allow for the counting of indirect and induced jobs, which expands the number of jobs that can be counted to meet the EB-5 program's minimum job creation requirement, increasing the amount of EB-5 capital available for individual projects. Because the regional center program requires renewal, it has become dependent upon short-term extensions in recent years, creating a lack of stability in the marketplace. Due to the ability to count indirect and induced jobs, about 95 percent of all EB-5 capital in recent years has flowed through regional centers.[2]

Modification to the law has stalled in recent years, but even if it picks up in the future, nobody can predict what those changes will entail, and few are optimistic that retrogression will be fixed. Most likely, greater restrictions will be placed on the maintenance of regional centers, increasing the regulatory cost burden for projects to comply with USCIS rules, which will also increase the minimum investment threshold. Developers could see the pool of potential investors shrink dramatically, but the amount of capital would potentially increase since the decrease of investors is likely proportionally less than the increase in capital contributed per investor.

---

2   Alana Semuels, "Should Congress Let Wealthy Foreigners Buy Green Cards?" *The Atlantic*, September 21, 2015, https://www.theatlantic.com/business/archive/2015/09/should-congress-let-wealthy-foreigners-buy-citizenship/406432/.

Additionally, the possibility of redefining TEAs by incentivizing rural projects creates the greatest hurdle to getting the industry on the same legislative page to support long-term renewal, since redefining TEAs will greatly change the overall focus of viable projects.

Consequently, developers feel uncertainty about going forward with their projects in case the law changes midstream. What if modification makes EB-5 unfeasible? For investors, this means their planned path to immigration could suddenly disappear after years of waiting.

THE ORIGIN OF RETROGRESSION

Prior to 2014, as EB-5 grew in popularity, the program ran freely. Rules seemed more or less arbitrary, and the government saw no reason to limit the visa cap for any specific country. Once EB-5 gained traction and caps were met, the arbitrary system no longer seemed fair, so rules changed such that no single country could take more than 7 percent of total visas. The House Committee on Appropriations has recently sought to ease or eliminate the 7 percent rule, but this change has yet to be implemented.

Unfortunately, China's 7 percent gets claimed in the first day of each fiscal year, with those first 700 places in line getting filled on October 1. Every other country has the rest of the year to casually use up their allotment of visas, but that leaves thousands of visas unclaimed. Instead of discarding these remaining visas, the US government allows Chinese investors to reenter the line to claim them at the end of the fiscal year.

Even with those extra visas available to Chinese investors, demand has increased the wait time to around fifteen years, straining the process to the breaking point. If escalation continues, the growing wait line could make EB-5 investment from China entirely unviable as either a means of immigration or an SOF for developers. Growth in emerging markets exacerbates the problem since there will be fewer unused visas from other countries for those in retrogression.

EARLY RELEASE AND BRIDGE FUNDING

The capital stack of a typical EB-5 project consists of 50 percent from a bank, 20 percent from developer equity, and the remaining 30 percent from EB-5 investors, which is the hardest piece for developers to obtain. If a developer needs to raise $25 million of EB-5 funding, they must locate fifty investors and convince them to invest $500,000 each. Raising that much money could take a year or longer, and then the developer has to wait for the bank to close the deal. Only then can they start building.

A lot can happen in that year. Who knows what might

happen to the economy? Who knows what might happen to the bank or to the developer's particular industry? If any of them experiences a downturn, the bank might decide to not fund the loan. In the end, the developer has money from fifty investors but can't build and can't create jobs unless all of the funding comes together at the same time.

Bridge financing provides a solution to this potential problem. A bridge loan allows the developer to access $25 million today and repay it over the course of a year or two, as the EB-5 investment is raised. This arrangement enables the developer to start the project, efficiently construct without interruption, and create jobs. Whether the project recruits one investor or fifty, it will be completed, and jobs will be created, so each EB-5 investor should receive a green card, with all of its significant benefits.

After wiring, funds enter an escrow account with "early release" terms and conditions. Typically, early release means some or all investor funds become available to the project upon filing of the I-526. To protect the investor, there is usually a holdback of some portion of investor funds (typically 20 percent) to create a pool of liquidity to refund the rare I-526 denial, or the developer may provide a guaranty of a return of capital upon an I-526 denial. Investors should take care to ascertain the financial strength of the party that is guaranteeing the return of capital to the investor in the event of a denial, as not all such guaranties are equal, let alone viable.

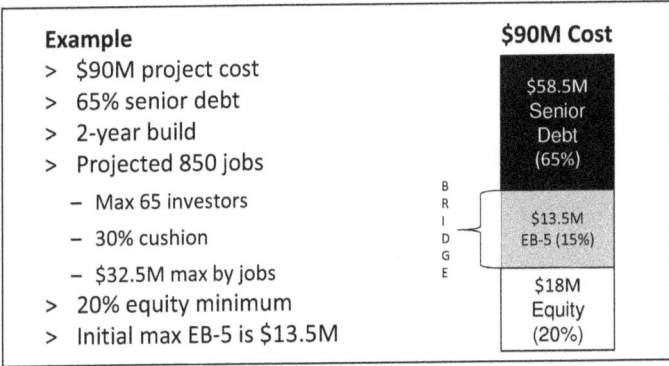

Example	$90M Cost
> $90M project cost	$58.5M Senior Debt (65%)
> 65% senior debt	
> 2-year build	
> Projected 850 jobs	
— Max 65 investors	$13.5M EB-5 (15%)
— 30% cushion	
— $32.5M max by jobs	$18M Equity (20%)
> 20% equity minimum	
> Initial max EB-5 is $13.5M	

(BRIDGE)

REDEPLOYED FUNDS

Traditionally, EB-5 investments are structured with a term of five years, though the documents usually provide for two one-year extensions to ensure that the investor funds can remain invested and "at risk" to satisfy the investment sustainment period required by USCIS. At the end of this period of time, all parties expect an exit event, such as a refinance or sale, to return investor capital and terminate the investment.

Because of retrogression, a Chinese investor might still have a three-year wait for their conditional visa and a two-year sustainment period, which creates a dilemma unforeseen by EB-5 projects taken to market before 2017. Premature return of capital before filing of the I-829 petition might result in a denial of the permanent green card. To prevent a potential denial, developers have resorted to redeploying the investor's money into other projects, which the investor may never have contemplated and which might create a securities compliance risk for the developer.

Adding to the confusion, there is no clear safe harbor definition of what constitutes "at risk." USCIS published the following subjective guidance on July 26, 2018:

> Once the job creation requirement has been met, the capital is properly at risk if it is used in a manner related to engagement in commerce (in other words, the exchange of goods or services) consistent with the scope of the new commercial enterprise's ongoing business. [29] After the job creation requirement is met, the following at-risk requirements apply:
>
> · The immigrant investor must have placed the required amount of capital at risk for the purpose of generating a return on the capital placed at risk;
> · There must be a risk of loss and a chance for gain; and
> · Business activity must actually be undertaken. [30]
>
> For example, if the scope of a new commercial enterprise was to loan pooled investments to a job-creating entity for the construction of a residential building, the new com-

mercial enterprise, upon repayment of a loan that resulted in the required job creation, may further deploy the repaid capital into one or more similar loans to other entities. Similarly, the new commercial enterprise may also further deploy the repaid capital into certain new issue municipal bonds, such as for infrastructure spending, as long as investments into such bonds are within the scope of the new commercial enterprise in existence at the time the petitioner filed the Immigrant Petition by Alien Entrepreneur (Form I-526).

Officers must determine whether further deployment has taken place, or will take place, within a commercially reasonable time and within the scope of the new commercial enterprise's ongoing business.[3]

Without a safe harbor definition, the redeployment of funds creates immigration risk for investors and a securities laws compliance risk for developers and regional centers.

Retrogression has created a paradigm in which developers are ready to exit and return capital within the originally intended period of five to seven years, but some or all of their Chinese investors have not yet even

---

3   *USCIS Policy Manual*, vol. 6, *Immigrants*, July 26, 2018, https://www.uscis.gov/policymanual/Print/PolicyManual-Volume6-PartG.html#footnote-31.

received their conditional green card. Project sponsors have three options:

1. Return the capital to the investor, which likely results in the denial of a green card as the investment would technically not overlap the two-year sustainment period after issuance of the conditional green card.

2. Allow liquid funds to remain on deposit within the New Commercial Enterprise, which raises the question of "at risk" and could expose investors to misappropriation of their funds.

3. Redeploy investor funds into another project to maintain the "at risk" requirement, which may give rise to issues with compliance with securities laws if redeployment and the subsequent project were not contemplated in the original securities offering.

When sourcing investment from China, or any other country that potentially may go into retrogression, the developer needs to create a structure that contemplates holding investor funds for an extended period in a manner that meets USCIS "at risk" requirements and is fully disclosed up front to the investor.

URBAN VERSUS RURAL PROJECTS

Current speculation suggests that legislative support for long-term EB-5 regional center legislation would include incentives for investors to consider rural investments over traditionally favored "gateway" markets, such as New York City, Miami, and Los Angeles. These incentives include redefining TEAs so that the lower-dollar investment threshold will not apply to most urban investments, or reserving "priority" green cards for investments made outside of gateway markets. Naturally, legislators are lining up to support their constituents and neither side shows any sign of compromise, which is the primary cause for the string of continuing resolutions without a long-term solution.

In anticipation, promoters have turned their attention to oil and gas wells, steel mills, and other projects in rural areas, betting that these projects will give their clients a potential advantage if legislation changes to favor such projects and can be applied retroactively.

"Invest in a rural project today, and you will get ahead of everyone else in line when the changes occur."

That's the claim, but nobody can predict exactly what legislative changes will take place, if and when they are finally enacted. Hope alone makes rural projects very attractive in China.

Failed legislation from March 2018 indicates this strategy was nearly spot-on. The legislation provided for approximately 3,000 "priority" visas based on rural or urban-distressed criteria and an opportunity for investors in existing projects that met these qualifications to adjust their status to the priority visa by increasing their investment to meet the newly set minimum investment of $925,000. Of course, taking advantage of this opportunity required two conditions:

1. That the investor had an additional $425,000 to risk.
2. That the project had the ability to legitimately deploy the additional funds to maintain the "at risk" requirement and the offering documents permitted acceptance of additional investment funds.

While the bill in March 2018 failed, it may be a leading indicator of what will happen on a future bill. New projects may incorporate flexibility into their offering documents to benefit from potential changes in legislation rather than becoming victims.

GETTING FUNDS OUT OF CHINA

Investors face a complex situation when attempting to wire money out of China. Wiring time has extended from a weeklong process to an average of forty-five days. Current rules cap wire transfers out of the country at US $50,000 per year, but for EB-5 to work, an investor has to wire at least $500,000, excluding administrative fees.

Recent restrictions from the Chinese government lower the cap for wire transfers down to $10,000, though these new restrictions have yet to be enforced.

Only investors who plan well could make it work, and it would require extensive work on the part of the investor and an immigration attorney. The volume of investment funds would almost certainly drop dramatically. This complexity drags the process out even longer and is yet another reason developers need a bridge loan.

ALTERNATE VISA ROUTES AND OBSTACLES

Many investors find EB-5 attractive because it provides an opportunity to place their children in American universities at domestic tuition rates, with eligibility for financial aid, which could be a return of over $20,000 annually if attending at resident tuition rates. Since retrogression takes up to fifteen years, the investment has to begin before the child is eight years old; otherwise, it won't be complete in time for that child to use the visa for school. If the investor starts later, then, as an alternative, the child can apply for a student visa, and the parents can gift funds to the student, who becomes the primary EB-5 applicant in order to stay in the US after graduation. If retrogression extends past graduation, the child can stay in school to earn an advanced degree or take English lessons for six months each year to remain on the student visa until the EB-5 process is complete. However, eventually a green card becomes necessary.

If a family starts the EB-5 process after their child relocates to the US on a student visa, then only broker-dealers can offer them an investment opportunity. US securities laws prevent foreign immigration agents from offering EB-5 to foreign individuals who are in the US.

Many different visa statuses provide US residency, but, like student visas, they are temporary, so investors need a permanent alternative. Student visas can usually be extended as long as education is pursued. Tourist visas typically last ninety days. H-1B visas can last longer, as long as the resident remains employed by someone who sponsors the visa based on specialized skills, leaving the foreign person beholden to their employer. However, current policy trends indicate a curtailment of the H-1B program, which may lead to a growth opportunity for EB-5, as H-1B visa holders seek a pathway to permanency.

Workers who have lived in the US for years, constantly renewing their H-1B, have set up a life in the US and want to stay. Also, workers who expect to stay past their student visas on H-1B might require an alternate route.

Many seek to enter the US with an L-1 visa, for short-term executive, management, and specialized work, and convert to an EB-1C permanent residency visa. However, this conversion often proves difficult because EB-1C is intended for executives at large corporations with significant job creation. It's not a path of investment like EB-5. Some agents market EB-1C as a viable alternative to EB-5, but unless it applies to the investor in a substantive way, they run an enormous risk of being denied.

Renewed concerns of nationalizing private assets have fueled the desire for immigration investment in China in the wake of the term limit repeal for the Chinese president, but retrogression has depressed demand for EB-5. Accordingly, Chinese agents have begun more aggressively marketing immigration investments to other countries to feed their machine. English-speaking countries that compete with the US for education, specifically Canada, Australia, and New Zealand, have become the first preference for alternatives to the US EB-5 program. However, those programs cost considerably more and have equally stringent SOF and screening processes. Next, agents have turned to Europe, chiefly Portugal, Cyprus, Malta, and Greece, which have favorable immigration laws. Finally, as a last alternative, agents have turned to Caribbean countries, a fast option for those who can't qualify for the more attractive options.

IMPACT ON DEVELOPERS SEEKING CAPITAL

China has been a highly efficient market to raise EB-5 capital, which has funded significant projects that increased the tax base of communities, created US jobs, and brought high-net- worth families to the US. The current state of retrogression has reduced the number of investors coming from China to a trickle and slowed the flow of development capital into the US.

Consequently, marketplaces outside of China have increased in importance. Larger regional centers and other EB-5 stakeholders around the world have already begun to establish relationships in other countries. Large projects requiring hundreds of investors can no longer rely on China as the sole source of investors, which creates an opportunity for smaller projects to get back into China. Further, with large regional centers spreading the EB-5 word throughout the New World, US-based developers with ties to those countries have a built-in marketing advantage to raise capital in those markets.

For that reason, EB-5 is going to the New World, and in this case, the New World consists of emerging markets.

CHAPTER TWO

THE NEW WORLD

Wealthy citizens in any country can generally create good living conditions for themselves and for their families, but they can't fix volatile economic conditions, an unstable government, or a lack of educational opportunity—not without emigrating to another country. This general trend occurs in nations experiencing a rise in EB-5 investors. People want to bring their families to a place with economic stability, more educational opportunities, and safer neighborhoods.

Potential Wait Time Until Visa Number Availability*

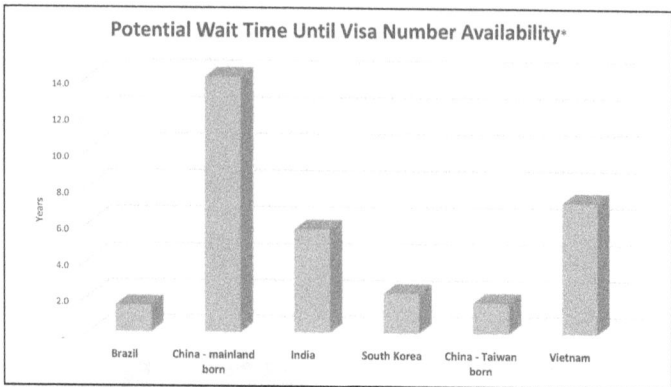

* Assumes filed Oct. 30, 2018 and includes estimated time to adjudicate the I-526 petition
Source: USCIS presentation to AILA/IIUSA Conference Chicago October 30, 2018

WHAT SETS THE US APART?

No matter the country of origin, the welfare of children and family remains the primary motivation for EB-5 investors. Individuals tend to endure all sort of problems, including political instability, pollution, and crime, when it only affects their own lives. They feel most comfortable in their home country because they know the culture and speak the language. Once children enter the picture, those same individuals become more aware of the dangers in their surrounding community and less willing to tolerate high risk. This creates strong motivation to seek better, safer opportunities.

Though many countries have much to offer an investor, the stability of the US economy, rule of law, and elite universities makes it the most ideal destination. China has shifted from substandard poverty conditions to become the second largest economy in the world within one generation, creating tremendous wealth in the middle class. People who are old enough to remember standing in breadlines in China are just now entering their sixties. These individuals know all too well how quickly an economy can completely transform, so they harbor concerns that it could reverse just as quickly. Residents of Aleppo, Syria know this in the most tragic way possible. Less than a generation ago, Aleppo thrived as an economic and cultural capital in Syria, and it now lies in utter ruins.

American cities do not have the same risks. Economic cycles come and go, of course, but compared to most of the rest of the world, the US offers consistent economic stability.

Let's examine a few key countries according to the most relevant criteria regarding EB-5.

INDIA

Most immigrants from India apply for H-1B visas, which allow US companies to employ foreign workers. In fact, India accounts for 80 percent of all H-1B visas. Under President George W. Bush, the number of H-1B visas doubled, which made the tech industry skyrocket. Since then, the H-1B visa limit has dropped back to historic levels, which has created a shortage of tech workers. The industry expects President Donald Trump to cut those numbers by as much as 50 percent in an attempt to force the industry to hire more American workers.

Whether or not he will actually slash the number of visas is just conjecture, but he has asked USCIS to scrutinize H-1B in order to make the approval process more difficult. In 2017, 190,000 people applied for H-1B, but already this year, the number has dropped to 165,000. If the number of visas gets cut, Indian citizens will lose their primary pathway to the US and competition for top H-1B spots will intensify, leaving EB-5 as the most reliable alternative, despite entering retrogression in October 2018.

POLITICAL SYSTEM RISK

India is a vastly populated nation and the largest democracy in the world. There is no political instability, but the government neither promotes nor encourages the EB-5 program.

THE RISE OF WEALTH

In recent years, there has been a dramatic rise of wealth in India. The country is home to roughly 245,000 millionaires, and total household wealth currently stands at $5 trillion.[4] By 2022, the number of millionaires is expected

---

4   "India Home to 245,000 Millionaires, Household Wealth at $5 Trillion: Report," Livemint, November 5, 2017, https://www.livemint.com/Money/O2U4eJpykOUQcwswFI8lRL/India-home-to-245000-millionaires-household-wealth-at-5-t.html.

to hit 372,000, with total household income growing to $7.1 trillion. When wealthy Indians immigrate to the United States, they bring much of that wealth with them and generate even more. Indians who live in the United States are among the wealthiest demographic in America.

EDUCATIONAL SYSTEM

In recent years, India has made significant progress on the quality of public education, boosting enrollment rates, though dropout rates remain a challenge.[5] In fact, India's improved education system is one of the main contributors to its economic development. Its higher education system is the third largest in the world, behind the United States and China, but many universities suffer from subpar quality and a lack of funding. For this reason, many Indian citizens look to the American university system as the best opportunity for their children.

ENVIRONMENTAL QUALITY

India has seen rapid development in the past two decades, but it has come at the cost of increasing pollution, particularly in industrial areas. Weak industrial regulation means factories do not follow strict pollution-control measures. The capital, Delhi, has some of the worst air

---

5   Urvashi Sahni, "Primary Education in India: Progress and Challenges,"
     Brookings, January 20, 2015, https://www.brookings.edu/research/
     primary-education-in-india-progress- and-challenges/.

quality on Earth, leading to an increase in respiratory and cardiovascular diseases.[6] American cities, by contrast, are subject to stringent clean air and water laws and provide healthier living conditions.

CRIME

Crime is not a particular problem in India. Many categories of crime are actually lower than in the United States.[7] Unlike many South American countries, a desire to escape high crime is not a motivating factor for potential EB-5 investors in India.

MOVING FUNDS OUT OF THE COUNTRY

Moving funds out of the country is relatively simple. An individual in India can move $250,000, so spouses could move the full $500,000 needed for an EB-5 investment. This makes investing in an EB-5 project much easier than in countries like China, where increasing restrictions have made wire transfers extremely challenging. Often, the challenge for funds coming from India is adequate documentation that the funds originated from a legal source and have been taxed by the government.

---

6   "India Cities Dominate World Air Pollution List." BBC, May 2, 2018, http://www.bbc.com/news/world-asia-india-43972155.

7   "Country vs Country: India and United States Compared: Crime Stats," NationMaster, accessed June 27, 2018, http://www.nationmaster.com/country- info/compare/India/United-States/Crime.

Wealth in India, as in many other countries, often consists of "gray money," funds earned legally but unreported to taxing authorities. Sourcing investment from India requires experienced immigration attorneys and SOF consultants to ensure adequate documentation for each investor.

MARKETING PREFERENCES

Because of India's entrepreneurial culture, investors prefer a project that feels active rather than passive. Cultural distinctions make them cautious, so they also prefer a smaller project where they can feel like participants. In fact, many investors prefer doing their own project with a few friends rather than investing in a large project. Indian investors tend to negotiate investment terms, including all costs and administrative fees.

OTHER CONSIDERATIONS

SEBI, the Securities and Exchange Board of India, regulates the securities market in India, similar to the US Securities and Exchange Commission. SEBI and the US government have joint agreements and work together to prevent fraud. This kind of cooperation does not exist in most countries.

In November 2016, India's leaders demonetized all 500-

and 1000-rupee banknotes in an attempt to curtail gray money and the so-called shadow economy. This resulted in cash shortages, which continue to be a problem despite government efforts to correct the problem in recent months.[8] For investors, the primary fear is currency devaluation, with the rupee showing signs of weakness.[9]

Even if the rupee regains strength, Indian investors tend to act far more cautiously than Chinese investors, which can create delays in the investment cycle. As a result, an opportunity that might look great on paper can stretch on for months. Despite these cultural challenges, many projects are going to India, and time will soon tell how the market reacts to the news that the potential wait time is now 5.7 years.

VIETNAM

Vietnam's growing economy has generated increased interest in EB-5, due largely to the rise of a wealthy class combined with a desire for greater opportunities.

---

8   Anto Antony and Anirban Nag, "Why India Is Now Scrambling to Print More Currency," *Bloomberg*, April 19, 2018, https://www.bloomberg.com/news/articles/2018-04-20/ why- india-is-now-scrambling-to-print-more-currency-quicktake.

9   PTI, "Investors Fear Weakening Rupee May Affect Solar Tariffs: Study," *Money Control*, May 16, 2018, https://www.moneycontrol.com/news/india/investors-fear-weakening- rupee-may-affect-solar-tariffs-study-2570027.html.

POLITICAL SYSTEM RISK

Vietnam is a communist country, with a government that tightly controls both its people and the flow of money. At any time, the government can seize property and assets. Like China, the risk is always there, even if the government is not currently acting on it.

THE RISE OF WEALTH

As of 2016, Vietnam had 12,000 millionaires, an increase of 354 percent over ten years.[10] Centimillionaires (those worth $100 million or more) in particular are on the rise. Communist Vietnam now has more millionaires than nearby capitalist countries like the Philippines.

EDUCATIONAL SYSTEM

Vietnam's government has been working hard to improve its state-run education system, but schools suffer from outdated curricula, teaching methods, and a lack of opportunities, particularly at the university level.[11] This creates further incentive for wealthy residents to invest in EB-5.

---

10 Vuong Duc Anh, "Vietnam Has over 12,000 USD Millionaires: Wealth Report," *VN Express*, April 30, 2016, https://e.vnexpress.net/news/business/vietnam-has-over-12-000-usd-millionaires-wealth-report-3395913.html.

11 Education in Vietnam," InterNations, accessed June 27, 2018, https://www.internations.org/vietnam-expats/guide/living-in-vietnam-15470/education-in-vietnam-3.

ENVIRONMENTAL QUALITY

Due to rapid development and deforestation, poor vehicle emission standards, and bad urban planning, the air quality in Vietnam has suffered in recent years.[12] Urban areas struggle with dirty water and poor waste treatment. Though the government is attempting to address these environmental concerns, many wealthy residents desire a cleaner and healthier place to live.

CRIME

Crime in Vietnam has been on the rise for the past three years.[13] Though crime against foreigners remains rare, wealthy citizens often feel targeted. Corruption and bribery are particular problems, making immigration to the US attractive for wealthy citizens.

MOVING FUNDS OUT OF THE COUNTRY

The Vietnamese government maintains a strong hold over the monetary system, making it particularly difficult for citizens to get money out of the country. In fact, getting the investor's money into the project creates the biggest hurdle for EB-5 investment in Vietnam.

---

12 "Vietnam—Environment," GlobalSecurity.org, accessed June 26, 2018, https://www.globalsecurity.org/military/world/vietnam/enviro.htm.

13 "Crime in Vietnam," Numbeo, accessed June 26, 2018, https://www.numbeo.com/crime/country_result.jsp?country=Vietnam.

MARKETING PREFERENCES

Similar to China, Vietnamese investors prefer the apparent reassurance of big, flashy projects attached to well-known brand names.

THE MIDDLE EAST

The Middle East contains numerous countries with wealthy potential EB-5 investors. Let's take a look at the major players.

TURKEY

Turkey has experienced significant political and social turmoil in recent years, though it continues to be recognized as a regional power. The nation remains an economic powerhouse, with the seventeenth largest GDP (gross domestic product) in the world.[14]

Turkey's currency, the lira, has plunged in value as part of an overall economic collapse, with the exchange rate expected to reach five lira to one dollar by the end of the year, a 30 percent decrease in the last twelve to eighteen months.

---

14 "The 20 Countries with the Largest Gross Domestic Product (GDP) in 2017 (in Billion U.S. dollars)," Statistica, accessed June 27, 2018, https://www.statista.com/statistics/268173/countries-with-the-largest-gross-domestic- product-gdp/.

Political System Risk

Turkey has an unstable government, creating strong incentive among its wealthy citizens to get out of the country. After the failed coup of 2016, President Erdogan asserted stronger control. People who supported the opposition party found themselves in a precarious situation. It has become very dangerous to speak out against the government, and the situation seems unlikely to change anytime soon. Recently, the government invaded Syria, creating further anxiety, which has contributed to the economic collapse.

The Rise of Wealth

Turkey has seen some of the largest outflow of wealth of any country in the world. In the last two years, 12,000 millionaires have fled the country.[15] This exodus of wealthy residents is due to worsening political, security, and economic problems.

Educational System

Turkish people tend to be more educated than people in other parts of the world, but the public education system

---

15 "Private wealth in Turkey in decline: Report." Hurriyet Daily News. http://www. hurriyetdailynews.com/private-wealth-in-turkey-in-decline-report-127983 (accessed June 26, 2018)

is becoming more overtly religious.[16] Still, education tends not to be the primary motivating factor for wealthy citizens fleeing the country.

Environmental Quality

Air pollution is becoming a bigger problem in Turkey's urban areas.[17] In fact, more than 97 percent of Turkey's urban population is exposed to an unhealthy amount of air pollution.

Crime

Overall crime rates have been on the rise in Turkey since the 1990s.[18] Since 2014, the country has seen a 400 percent increase in drug-related crimes, theft, and murder. This provides strong incentive for wealthy citizens to find a safer place to live and raise their children.

IRAN

With the world's second largest natural gas supply and

---

16 Shaheen, Kareem. The Guardian. "'They want a devout generation': how education in Turkey is changing." https://www.theguardian.com/world/2017/sep/20/devout- generation-education-turkey-changing (accessed June 25, 2018)

17 Brett Smith, "Turkey: Environmental Issues, Policies and Clean Technology," AZOCleanTech. com, September 10, 2015, https://www.azocleantech.com/article.aspx?ArticleID=571.

18 "Turkey 2018 Crime & Safety Report: Ankara," United States Department of State, Bureau of Diplomatic Security, March 26, 2018, https://www.osac.gov/Pages/ContentReportDetails. aspx?cid=23755.

fourth largest fossil fuel reserves, Iran has become a major regional economic power.[19] Nevertheless, ongoing political tensions over the country's nuclear program have resulted in international sanctions, which have ramped up recently.

Political System Risk

For Iranians, the primary appeal for leaving the country comes down to government instability and political tension. However, hostility between the Iranian and US governments creates an extra layer of challenge for Iranian citizens interested in the EB-5 program. Iran is on the Trump travel ban list, so even if investors get approved, it's unlikely they will earn a visa.

The Rise of Wealth

Tehran alone contains 14,000 high-net-wealth individuals and 720 millionaires, so living the good life is quite possible in Iran,[20] evidenced in part by the growth of plastic surgery, with over 40,000 procedures performed

---

19 EIA, "Iran Energy Profile: Holds Some of World's Largest Deposits of Proved Oil and Natural Gas Reserves," Eurasia Review, May 18, 2018, https://www.eurasiareview. com/18052018-iran-energy-profile-holds-some-of-worlds- largest-deposits-of-proved-oil-and-natural-gas-reserves-analysis/

20 Lubna Hamdan, "Revealed: Top Mideast Cities for Millionaires," Arabian Business, April 30, 2015, http://www.arabianbusiness.com/revealed-top-mideast-cities-for-millionaires- 591021. html.

each year.[21] However, the current US administration's sanctions against Iran threaten to send the economy into a recession, creating extra incentive for the wealthy to leave the country as soon as possible.

Educational System

Iran has above-average literacy rates, and public education benefited from a five-year government development plan that lasted from 2005 to 2010. Public universities are also tuition-free. As a result, educational opportunities do not tend to be a motivating factor for Iranian investors.

Environmental Quality

Urban areas in Iran suffer from poor air quality. Tehran suffers from some of the highest pollution levels in the world, leading to a spike in respiratory disease. Some days, air pollution in Tehran is so bad, schools are closed down.[22]

---

21   AFP, "Iran Leaps into World's Top 10 Countries Performing Plastic Surgery," The National, January 24, 2016, https://www.thenational.ae/arts-culture/iran-leaps-into-world-s-top-10-countries-performing-plastic-surgery-1.174897.

22   "Choking Level of Air Pollution in Tehran Shuts Down Schools," Telesur, December 17, 2017, https://www.telesurtv.net/english/news/Choking-Levels-of-Air-Pollution-in-Tehran-Shuts-Schools--20171217-0023.html.

Crime

Crime, particularly in Tehran,[23] has been on the rise in recent years. In particular, illegal drug use is rampant, but corruption is also a problem at all levels of society. Despite this, the crime rate does not seem to be a major reason for investors to leave the country.

Moving Funds out of the Country

The biggest problem with transferring money from Iranian investors is not their ability to get the money out but the fact that US banks won't accept it. Though US banks have no government restrictions preventing them from accepting Iranian money, the compliance cost is high due to complex regulations resulting from ongoing political tensions.

SAUDI ARABIA

The Kingdom of Saudi Arabia is well-known as the world's largest producer and exporter of oil, and it has become one of the major economies in the world. As a result, there are many wealthy citizens.

---

23   "Crime in Tehran, Iran." Numbeo, last updated October 2018, https://www.numbeo.com/crime/in/Tehran.

Political System Risk

The political and legal situation in Saudi Arabia is unique in that non-Saudi residents are forced to leave the country once they reach retirement age. Even people who have lived and worked in the country for decades are required to leave. The purpose of this law is to keep non-Saudis from becoming a burden on the system, but older wealthy non-Saudi citizens have to look for somewhere to live. This could make EB-5 investment attractive.

The Rise of Wealth

Saudi Arabia has the most millionaires of any country in the Middle East, and that number is on the rise. Most recent figures put the number of millionaires at over 176,000.[24]

Educational System

Saudi Arabia has seen the largest percentage-based increase in students coming to the United States to attend college. The desire for quality higher education is perhaps the primary motivation for people leaving the country.

---

24   Greg Wilcox, "Middle East Millionaire Club Grows as Combined Riches Top $2.42 Trillion," Arab News, September 29, 2017, http://www.arabnews.com/node/1169346/middle-east.

Environmental Quality

Urbanization has led to an increase in air and water pollution, a situation made all the more severe by the high level of oil extraction taking place across the country.

Crime

The crime rate in Saudi Arabia remains lower than that of many developed nations. Recent increases have been attributed to a higher number of foreign workers, but this does not appear to be a motivating factor for people seeking to leave the country.

Moving Funds out of the Country

There is no limit to the amount of money that can be transferred out of the country, so long as that money is earned from legal business activity. Investors only get in trouble if they attempt to wire more money than they have legally earned, in which case authorities might open an investigation.[25]

NICHE EXAMPLES

Sometimes countries experience a short but significant spike in interest in EB-5. Egypt during the Arab

---

25   "What Is the Limit to Transfer Money from Saudi Arabia?" Life in Saudi Arabia, accessed June 27, 2018, http://lifeinsaudiarabia.net/blog/2016/09/07/what-is-limit-to-transfer- money-fro/.

Spring serves as a perfect example. The Coptic Christian religious minority dealt with a lot of discrimination, including acts of vandalism and violence. This caused a spike in interest, but it has since gone away.

In Dubai, the indigenous population is not particularly interested in leaving the country, but the country has a growing population of nonresident, wealthy Indians who have come to the country to do business. Dubai also provides a safe place for Iranians to invest in EB-5. It's not possible to market an EB-5 project in Iran, and it's not possible to meet with Iranian investors there. Instead, marketing and meetings must occur in a neutral country like Dubai, which serves as an international hub for people from all over the Middle East. People conduct weekend EB-5 seminars in world-class hotels across Dubai for this very reason.

LATIN AMERICA

Political and economic instability exists in many Latin American countries, typically related to the potential nationalization of assets, currency deflation, and economic volatility. As in China, most Latin American EB-5 investors see the program as a way to bring their children to the US. For some, American educational opportunities create a powerful incentive. Most EB-5 funds from Latin America go to projects in South Florida, where many Latin American citizens have family or cultural ties.

BRAZIL

Brazil is now one of the top four markets for EB-5 investors, behind China. A number of social and economic factors have contributed to this.

Political System Risk

Corruption is widespread in Brazilian politics, especially overbilling for services and bribery.[26] This affects every level of government, from local politics all the way to the national government.

The Rise of Wealth

Despite economic woes, there has been a significant increase in the number of millionaires in Brazil in recent years, with the current total of 164,000 expected to increase to 296,000 in the next five years.

Educational System

Brazilian students underperform in subjects like reading, math, and science, though there has been a slight improvement since 2000.[27] There are 2,600 public

---

26   Maira Martini, "The Real Cost of Corruption in Brazil," Voices for Transparency, December 22, 2017, https://voices.transparency.org/the-real-cost-of-corruption-in-brazil-f3def6d17c94.

27   "Brazil," Pisa 2015, accessed June 28, 2018, http://www.compareyourcountry.org/pisa/country/BRA.

and private universities across the country. Still, many wealthy Brazilians seek better options for their children.

Environmental Quality

Brazil has famously struggled with deforestation, but the government has implemented numerous environmentally friendly initiatives in recent years, embracing sustainable foresting. Nevertheless, Rio de Janeiro and São Paulo are among the top 100 most polluted cities in the world.[28]

Crime

The crime rate in Brazil, particularly violent crime, has skyrocketed, placing the country in the top twenty for homicide rates. Recently, crime has gotten so bad that Brazil has begun to rely on soldiers to keep the peace rather than the police.[29] High crime rates are the primary motivating factor for wealthy residents looking to leave the country. São Paulo has one of the highest rates of helicopter ownership of any major city, with more than 400 helicopters making 1,300 trips a day as wealthy residents take to the skies to avoid crime and traffic. The

---

28 "Pollution Index 2018," Numbeo, accessed June 27, 2018, https://www.numbeo.com/pollution/rankings.jsp.

29 Marcelo Sayao, "Brazil Is Relying on Soldiers Instead of Regular Police—Here's Why," The Conversation, March 15, 2017, http://theconversation.com/brazil-is-relying-on-soldiers- instead-of-regular-police-heres-why-73034.

city also has more armored cars than any other city in the world, with around 140,000 retrofitted vehicles in use.[30] A desire to live and raise children in safety creates perhaps the strongest incentive for wealthy residents to leave the country.

Moving Funds out of the Country

Moving money out of Brazil is both difficult and expensive.[31] Brazilian bank processes tend to be slow and cumbersome, and only BRL$9,999 (equivalent to about US$2,806) can be transferred in a single month.

VENEZUELA

A major oil-producing nation, Venezuela has been wracked with political and economic turmoil in recent years. There are many reasons why a wealthy citizen might want to leave the country, but doing so will prove difficult.

Political System Risk

Venezuela is in the midst of an historic political and eco-

---

30   Leonardo Sakamoto, "The Future of São Paulo Sleeps in an Improvised Shack," The Guardian, November 27, 2017, https://www.theguardian.com/cities/2017/nov/27/ sao- paulo-future-inequality-occupations-homeless-movements-mtst-workers.

31   "Getting Money Out of Brazil," Rio Travel, September 19, 2016, http://www.riotravel.net/blog/ getting-money-out-of-brazil/id/8.

nomic crisis. Heavily disputed elections, extreme food shortages, and an increasingly authoritarian president have greatly contributed to widespread misery across the country. This creates a strong incentive for wealthy residents to flee the country.

The Rise of Wealth

Sadly, because of the economic chaos, Venezuela is suffering from hyperinflation. Millionaires who manage to leave the country with their wealth intact tend to head to places like Miami and Los Angeles.

Educational System

The poor and middle class in Venezuela struggle just to get enough to eat, so education simply is not the biggest priority for most people. Students are at risk due to political violence, and teachers struggle to make ends meet.[32] This certainly provides a strong incentive for wealthy citizens with families.

Environmental Quality

Water pollution is the number one environmental problem in Venezuela. The dumping of industrial waste has

---

32   Reese Erlich, "Venezuela's Crisis Takes a Toll on Education," Deutsche Welle, May 15, 2017, http://www.dw.com/en/venezuelas-crisis-takes-a-toll-on-education/a-38858211.

damaged the coastline. Air pollution is also a rampant problem in the capital region.[33]

Crime

Despite a fierce crackdown on crime, Venezuela has been ranked as the least safe country in the world due to a surge in violence.[34] Crime has become a full-blown crisis, creating a strong incentive for wealthy residents to get their families out of the country.

Moving Funds out of the Country

It's extremely difficult to get money out of Venezuela, especially if that money is in a Venezuelan bank. Wealthy citizens looking to move money out of the country might have to cross the border into another country to do so.

Marketing Preferences

Venezuelan investors are chiefly looking for a fast way out of the country, as economic and political woes con-

---

33 "The 10 Most Important Environmental Problems in Venezuela," Life Persona, February 7, 2018, https://www.lifepersona.com/ the-10-most-important-environmental-problems- in-venezuela.

34 Jim Wyss, "In Venezuela, People Fear the Night, and the Cops Are Not Much Help, Study Shows," Miami Herald, August 3, 2017, http://www.miamiherald.com/news/nation- world/ world/americas/venezuela/article165057502.html.

tinue. A project that can move relatively quickly will be of greatest interest.

MEXICO

With the fifteenth largest GDP in the world, Mexico has a strong economy, though that economy is linked to intra-North American trade, which will now be dependent on the recently negotiated US-Mexico-Canada Agreement. Wealthy Mexican citizens tend to have personal ties to the US, which should make EB-5 an attractive option for gaining a green card.

Political System Risk

Political corruption is one of the biggest problems in Mexico. Embezzlement, extortion, and bribery are rampant at all levels and in every branch of government.[35] Wealthy citizens, in particular, are targeted.

The Rise of Wealth

After Donald Trump's election, the Mexican economy experienced a brief downturn. This only lasted a few months, and the economy has since bounced back. Mexico is once again a strong market. Many Mexican

---

35   Luis Rubio, "Corruption Is Mexico's Original Sin," Foreign Policy, December 26, 2017, http://foreignpolicy.com/2017/12/26/corruption-is-mexicos-original-sin/.

citizens have strong personal and financial ties to the United States. In many instances, they already own homes in the US, so they are simply looking for a legal form of immigration.

At one time, it was common for wealthy Mexican immigrants living in the US, particularly in Texas, to invite family to come and live with them. Many would enter on tourist visas and then simply remain past the expiration date. When the US government caught on to this tactic, they began denying entry to many Mexican citizens. Mexican citizens who return home often cannot return to the US, even though their spouses and children have been living in the country for years. This widespread family separation creates a strong incentive to find a legal way to get back into the United States.

Educational System

Millions of children in Mexico lack access to a quality education.[36] Mexican president Enrique Peña Nieto made education reform a flagship policy, but the situation changed very little. Many parents long to bring their children into the United States to give them access to good schools.

---

36 Nina Lakhani, "'The Help Never Lasts': Why Has Mexico's Education Revolution Failed?" The Guardian, August 15, 2017, https://www.theguardian.com/inequality/2017/aug/15/the-help-never-lasts-why-has- mexicos-education-revolution-failed.

Environmental Quality

Mexico is suffering from pollution due to factory discharge and industrial waste dumping.[37] A landmark climate change law was passed in 2012, but the government has been slow to implement it fully. Air pollution is particularly bad in Mexico City.

Crime

Rampant crime and gang activity make the headlines frequently in Mexico. Ruthless turf wars between drug cartels have resulted in countless civilian casualties, creating a strong incentive for Mexican families to cross the border into safer US cities.[38]

Moving Funds out of the Country

Transferring money from Mexico into the United States is relatively easy and very common. Numerous banks and transfer companies provide convenient services, though limits vary from bank to bank.

---

37 Jackson Rodriguez, "7 Environmental Problems in Mexico Very Serious," Life Persona, September 5, 2017, https://www.lifepersona.com/7-environmental-problems-in-mexico-very-serious.

38 "Mexico's Crime and Lack of Punishment," Financial Times, March 23, 2018, https://www.ft.com/content/ca4fc57a-2e97-11e8-9b4b-bc4b9f08f381.

THE PAPER TRAIL

No matter the investor's country of origin, USCIS applications require a significant paper trail to prove the source and path of all funds for a project. An investor must provide evidence that their investment is paid for with funds that were obtained legally and entered the US through legal pathways. If an investor receives a Request for Evidence (RFE), it indicates that the USCIS is looking at the file and has run into some kind of question or concern. If no evidence or clarification can be provided by the investor or if what is provided is not deemed suitable, the investor will receive a Notice of Intent to Deny (NOID). From there, a remedy must be found, or the investor's application will be denied. Some investors carry longer paper trails than others, but all projects are fraught with complexity and risk.

The SOF for an investor is critical to EB-5 project sponsors, as projects commonly offer to guarantee a return of investor capital in the event their I-526 is denied by USCIS. What made China attractive for many years was that Chinese agents had a clear idea of what was needed for the paper trail, so they handled it efficiently. As the industry branches out into other countries, emerging markets lack the same infrastructure. Adequately documenting the SOF becomes challenging, a situation that is further exacerbated due to the fact that many businesses in emerging markets are structured in such a way as to avoid taxation.

This complexity can be handled by immigration attorneys, though they do not typically enjoy this kind of work. An alternative is to outsource it to a consultant or CPA firm that can prepare all documentation for the investors to ensure approval. This is particularly helpful when the firm or consultant has an in-country presence and understands the best SOF strategies for investors from that country. The best SOF strategy is situationally dependent for each investor, based on how their funds were obtained and their country of origin.

CHAPTER THREE

ADAPTING INVESTMENT STRUCTURES IN A DYNAMIC MARKET

In theory, developers can pursue EB-5 financing for almost any type of project, but what is possible under program rules is not always marketable. Without investor demand, developers will struggle to obtain funding. When considering EB-5 for a project, the developer must understand the factors that motivate investors. For example, construction projects in gateway communities traditionally generate the most interest, while speculative tech startups have historically drawn the least.

Ultimately, EB-5 investors care more about the relative certainty of job creation to achieve their green card objective and return of capital, and far less about a financial yield on the investment. A developer can promote the next Facebook or Uber, promising an astronomical return, without getting a second glance from the EB-5 market, because investors typically desire construction jobs and hard assets to back up their two primary investment objectives, which reduces their perception of risk. However, boutique project sponsors with a direct tie to a country (e.g., a Brazilian condo developer in Miami) can enhance their offering by adding EB-5 funds.

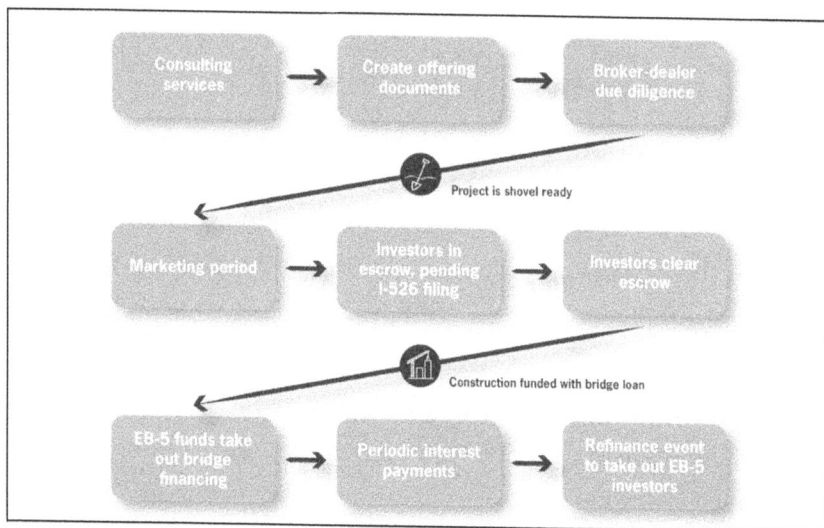

TANGIBLE AND FAMILIAR INVESTMENTS

Commercial real estate makes up the vast majority of all EB-5 investments. Frequently recurring projects include hotels, assisted living facilities, condos, apartment buildings, and mixed-used buildings. Not only do these projects provide hard assets with collateral for the investment, but they feel familiar to investors and appeal to the emotional side of selecting an investment. Despite cultural differences, investors all over the world have stayed in hotels. They understand the need for assisted living because every family deals with aging relatives. They have probably bought or leased an apartment or condo at some point. Even from thousands of miles away, investors in any country relate to these kinds of projects.

On the other hand, exotic projects like green technology, artificial intelligence, and space programs typically fail to generate much interest because investors lack familiarity or an intuitive connection with these kinds of projects. Investors often shy away from what they do not understand. By the same token, famous brand names inspire trust and familiarity, as does a tried-and-true concept with a proven track record. Familiarity inspires confidence.

Likewise, investors prefer projects in relatable geographic areas. Just as someone from the US might have no idea where the city of Jinan is located in China, regardless of the seven million people who live there, a Chinese investor probably has no idea where Macon, Georgia or Charlotte, North Carolina are located. They know New York City, LA, and Miami, so projects in these gateway cities tend to draw more interest.

Previously proposed legislation provides incentives intended to "level the playing field" by giving investors incentive to invest in manufacturing, infrastructure, or projects outside of gateway cities. These incentives include a lower investment amount and the ability for investors from retrogressed countries to move to the front of the line, which likely would make these the fastest-selling projects. If such legislated incentives passed, cattle farms, steel mills, and oil and gas wells would gain traction and potentially outpace commercial real estate. The potential of such changes is discussed in Chapter 4.

Unless legislative changes enhance access to EB-5 capital or address the problem of retrogression, demand in China will continue to decrease. Developers seeking capital in emerging markets are discovering that cultural differences require them to adjust investment structures to enhance the marketability of their projects in those respective countries.

ENHANCING MARKETABILITY

While several hundred projects are in the market at any given moment, only a few have the attributes that savvy investors desire, and even fewer meet all qualifications to make them worthy of consideration. Very few elite projects offer most or all of the features listed below that enhance the investor's attraction to the project.

- **Experienced development team.** Investors making an EB-5 investment to achieve a green card are not likely to bet on an inexperienced developer. To ensure marketability, the developer and integral partners need to be highly experienced, well-capitalized, have hard equity in the project, and possess a track record of successful development of similar projects.

- **An independent manager of the New Commercial Enterprise.** A relatively new but important differentiator is the use of a New Commercial Enterprise manager who is independent from the project developer. Prior fraud cases have involved misappropriation of funds because there was no independent oversight ensuring investor funds were used for the purpose stated in the offering materials. The use of a responsible party separate from the project gives investors the assurance that an accountable person with a fiduciary duty to the investors will act in their best interests to aggressively protect their immigration and return-of-capital objectives.

- **Use of an escrow agent.** The increased use of "early release" escrow terms has eroded the value of an investment escrow account, though there is still some value in the updated double escrow with drawdown. When USCIS processing times were under a year, many projects kept investor funds in escrow until their I-526 form was approved. While mildly inconvenient, this policy gave investors comfort that their funds were safe and fully refundable in the event their I-526 petition was rejected. As processing times increased, it became impractical to wait eighteen to twenty-four months before accessing investor funds, leading to early release with features such as I-526 denial insurance, holdback, or guaranty. Insurance policies that promised a return of capital in the event of a denial had brief popularity but quickly faded given the cost of the premium and concerns over the quality of the issuer. The "holdback" strategy retains 10 to 20 percent of the investors' capital in escrow to provide a pool of liquidity to refund a denied investor—basically self-insurance—with the reserve released as I-526 forms are approved. The denial guaranty typically comes from the developer, who can draw 100 percent of the investment funds upon filing of the I- 526 and commit to refunding the investment if the investor is denied for reasons other than fraud or misrepresentation. Investors should diligently read the fine print and understand the financial backing of those responsible for funding the denial guaranty to return their capital. All guarantors are not equal.

- **Relies heavily on construction jobs.** EB-5 requires the creation of ten new jobs for US persons for each investor. USCIS recognizes three types of jobs: direct, indirect, and induced. Direct jobs are those persons actually employed by the project upon completion (e.g., a hotel manager, front desk staff, and housekeeping at a hotel operation). Indirect jobs are those caused by the supply chain of the project, like the construction jobs created to build a hotel, or the support companies, such as linen washing companies in an operating hotel. Induced jobs are the economic "ripple effect" from the operation of the project (e.g., the food supplier to a new restaurant or jobs created through the local spending of employees of the project). Operational jobs pose a risk to an EB-5 investor, as those jobs are subject to the economy and financial performance of the project. A down economy might result in workforce reductions and lower financial performance, which will negatively impact the job creation analysis. However, construction jobs are calculated on the capital and time spent to build the project. An economist will generate a report using an econometric model and methods accepted by USCIS to certify the jobs created. Construction jobs pose the lowest risk to investors since those jobs will be deemed to be "created" so long as the project funds are spent and the project is built. An offshoot of relying on job creation is to ensure that the developer is providing a completion guaranty to ensure they will fund any change-orders or cost overruns to ensure completion of the project and the related job creation. Similar to a denial guaranty, the investor should investigate the financial wherewithal of the developer to support the completion guaranty. Finally, the project should project a healthy job creation cushion of 30 percent or more to meet market expectations.

- **Strong demand generator, preleasing, or presales.** Even though investors tend to take comfort in the familiarity of a development they can identify with, real estate development by its very nature is highly speculative. To reduce risk and enhance marketability, strong projects are located near a strong demand generator and go to market with high-level preleasing or presales to demonstrate market acceptance. Examples of demand generators include a hotel adjoining a conference center or airport, or student housing near a prestigious college campus. Retail or office projects with preleasing to tenants with a strong credit rating also demonstrate market acceptance and financial feasibility.

- **Sponsor equity of 20 percent or more.** EB-5 investors are motivated by getting a green card and a return of their capital. They seek projects where the sponsor has meaningful "skin in the game" to provide a downside cushion if the project is not as successful as forecasted. Projects with a healthy level of equity have a marketing advantage.

- **EB-5 funds are fully bridged with a temporary loan.** In a market where raising EB-5 capital has become increasingly challenging and takes a longer period of time, highly marketed projects employ bridge financing to begin construction and ensure a full capital stack to keep construction on time, with certainty of completion. Investors hesitate to invest in a project that has to achieve a minimal level of EB-5 funding in order to break ground. Few investors want to be "the first" and wait in escrow until enough other investors come along to start construction. Projects that can market while under construction and demonstrate funding for full completion without raising the maximum amount of EB-5 capital target have a marketing edge, though developers should be comfortable with the projected returns using bridge financing in the event all of the EB-5 capital sought is not ultimately sourced. Before undertaking this strategy, project sponsors should work with an experienced consultant and counsel to minimize the potential for USCIS to issue a Request for Evidence (RFE), which will delay approval of an exemplar filing and slow marketing momentum.

- **Construction is underway.** Projects that use a bridge and have meaningful construction underway when they go to market have an edge because they can estimate the number of jobs already created based on construction funds spent and progress to date. Investors are generally allocated jobs on a "first-in, first-out" basis, so early investors in a fully bridged project under construction essentially already know that their jobs have already been created—a significant marketing advantage.

- **Strong, viable exit strategy to return investor capital.** All investors want their capital returned at the appointed time, and a savvy investor will examine the feasibility of a project's exit strategy. The exit strategy for condos is clear: the sale of condo units. For other projects, it's not always so clear. Investors should always scrutinize the independent market study that accompanies the offering materials and EB-5 business plan submitted to USCIS, focusing in particular on the geographic and price-point submarkets, the completion within each, proposed projects yet to break ground, existing inventory, and other factors to get comfortable with the sale of inventory to return their capital.

As the EB-5 industry expands beyond China to emerging markets, cultural differences become evident. The Chinese model does not universally transfer to other countries. While financial returns were not material to Chinese EB-5 investors, returns matter significantly more in countries like India, where smaller projects that offer a small preferred rate of return and modest profit participation are favored over large, passive institutional projects that offer a meager yield.

In Latin America, projects are going to market offering the option for investors to purchase a "market rate" investment unit. This gives investors the opportunity to achieve a higher blended yield with a unit that has a below-market yield (the EB-5 unit) with a unit or units that return a yield closer to what one would expect from a private placement in development real estate. This approach gives investors an opportunity to diversify their currency risk by allocating some of their market-rate investment portfolio to a US-dollar-denominated investment.

The fifteen-year retrogression backlog in China has created a strong ripple effect on the entire market. Despite growing demand in China for immigration investment, the fifteen- year wait has depressed demand for EB-5, and the market in China is looking to the immigration investment programs of other countries. With diminishing supply in China, the EB-5 market is developing emerging markets, which is increasing the cost and time to raise funds. Cutting into the supply of unused visas outside of China ensures that Chinese retrogression will not improve without Congressional intervention.

With China effectively closed, higher quality projects that could obtain domestic funding likely will seek it in the US, as sourcing EB-5 financing in emerging markets provides little marginal value due to the time, cost, and complication. Under current market conditions, the overall quality of EB-5 investments will decline as projects without domestic options will seek EB-5, which makes the role of independent managers and broker-dealers extremely important to protect the integrity of the EB-5 capital market.

In Part 2 of this book, we will delve into attempts at long-term legislated solutions, integrity measures, and compliance requirements designed to protect the EB-5 program stakeholders, especially investors.

PART TWO

ATTEMPTS AT LONG-TERM RENEWAL

The Employment-Based Fifth Preference Program (EB-5) was enacted by Congress in 1990 as a way to stimulate foreign investment in the US economy and create jobs. The program was amended by Congress in 1993 with the Immigrant Investor Pilot Program (IIPP), which allowed foreign investors to put their money into so-called regional centers. This made it easier for investors to meet the program's job creation requirements.

Initial interest was disappointing, with program participation falling dramatically between 1999 and 2004. The
drop in applicants occurred as a result of rulings by the
Administrative Appeals Office of the Immigration and
Naturalization Service (INS) meant to create uniformity
in the program that instead made regulations more difficult for investors.

In 2001, a ruling in the United States Court of Appeals,
Tenth Circuit, in the case of U.S. v. O'Connor revealed rampant fraudulent investment schemes being perpetrated in
the EB-5 program. Wire fraud, immigration fraud, and
money laundering cast the whole program in a bad light,
which caused a decline in participation. The low point
came in 2003, when only seventy-one visas were issued.

In 2002, Congress attempted to reform the program by
passing the 21st Century Department of Justice Appropriations Authorization Act, which created important
regulatory guidance and eased some of the restrictive
regulations for investors. EB-5 regulations today are, in
fact, the result of statutory amendments made at that
time. Interest in the EB-5 program surged as a direct result
of the economic crisis of 2008. Bank financing became
more difficult, so developers began to look for alternative
sources of financing, which put EB-5 on their radar.

In both 2015 and 2017, Congress passed appropriations

legislation that temporarily extended the EB-5 Regional Center Program, but long-term reform has yet to be achieved. In April of 2018, Kathy Kovarik of the USCIS Office of Policy and Strategy declared her department's intention to get EB-5 regulatory reform completed this year. Invest in the USA (IIUSA), the national trade association for the EB-5 Regional Center Program, sent an open letter to USCIS encouraging the agency to finalize proposed EB-5 regulation, but with lower investment amounts ($1 million, or $800,000 in a TEA) than previously suggested.[39] It remains to be seen how this will play out, but legislative efforts are currently stalled, and the outlook appears bleak.

Although the program has bipartisan support, the ongoing controversy around immigration makes the future uncertain.

THE KEY STAKEHOLDERS—WHY CAN'T WE ALL JUST GET ALONG?

Let's take a look at the key constituents in the EB-5 process.

DEVELOPERS AND ISSUERS

Real estate developers serve as the primary consumers

---

39   "Regulations Update (8/2018?)," EB-5 Blog, May 9, 2018, https://blog.lucidtext.
      com/2018/05/09/regulations-update-august-2018/.

of EB-5 funds since they receive the investment. Developers often choose to use EB-5 funding to replace more expensive mezzanine debt or preferred equity, which have a high cost of capital (10 to 17 percent) when compared to an average EB-5 rate (5 to 7 percent). Developers may also seek EB-5 funding to replace comparably priced senior debt in order to obtain nonrecourse terms from the bank by using senior debt to fund a smaller portion of the capital stack or by offering an outright first mortgage and funding without a bank. The combination of a low cost and cash-flow savings (EB-5 is structured as interest-only payments) creates a significant incentive for developers to pursue EB-5.

To be competitive in the EB-5 market, developers should ensure that their project is located in an eligible TEA. USCIS recognizes two types of TEAs, high-unemployment areas (unemployment of 1.5 times the national average or higher) and rural areas (any area not within a metropolitan statistical area). Projects in a TEA qualify for a lower investment threshold, currently $500,000 versus $1,000,000, which provides a marketing advantage over projects that aren't in a TEA.

After confirming TEA eligibility, the developer should engage an economist to determine a preliminary count of EB-5 qualifying jobs, which will determine the upper limit of EB-5 capital since ten jobs must be created per investor. (Note: under the regional center context, EB-5 qualifying jobs are model-driven.) This allows the developer to count jobs associated with both construction expenditures and ongoing operations of the project. When determining the optimal amount of capital to raise, developers typically add a cushion of 30 to 40 percent for marketability and ensure at least 20 percent equity. For example, 1,400 projected jobs can technically support $70 million of EB-5 funds in a TEA at $500,000 per investor, but with a 40 percent cushion the amount of EB-5 capital would be $50 million, subject to maintaining 20 percent equity for marketability.

Once a developer decides to move forward on a project, a consultant is needed to prepare a business plan that addresses the unique eligibility requirements of USCIS, which are called "Matter of Ho." An experienced EB-5 consultant will also ensure that the project meets evolving USCIS trends that might impact the structure of the offering. Best practices recommend engaging a broker-dealer at this stage to consult on the investment structure for marketability and securities laws compliance. Concurrently, the developer works with their securities attorney to create a private placement memorandum (PPM) to market equity in the New Commercial Enterprise (also called the "issuer"), which includes numerous exhibits, such as a limited partnership agreement that defines the terms of the investment.

The issuer has a fiduciary duty to act in the best interests of the EB-5 investors to achieve their immigration objective and a return of capital. Competent issuers have a strong working knowledge of USCIS policies, procedures, and the constantly evolving interpretations of those rules. Likewise, the issuer must have a strong working knowledge of fund management, including escrow administration, project funding procedures, asset management, investor communications, and default resolution in case the project's Job Creating Entity should falter.

Historically, the general partner or manager of the New Commercial Enterprise has been affiliated with the Job Creating Entity, but this structure creates a significant conflict of interest as the lender and borrower are managed by related parties. This lack of third-party control has been the primary contributing factor in most fraud cases to date in EB-5.[40] Current best practices use a manager who is independent in all respects from the parties developing, owning, or managing the Job Creating Entity.

After completing the offering documents, an immigration attorney will review the entire package for compliance with immigration laws, while the broker-dealer reviews

---

40 Reid Thomas, "Common Risk Factors in EB-5 Fraud Cases," EB5 Investors Magazine, January 19, 2017, http://www.eb5investors.com/magazine/article/ common-risk-factors- eb5-fraud-cases.

for compliance, completes due diligence, and prepares a marketing plan. The immigration attorney then files an I-924 exemplar, which prompts USCIS to underwrite the project for compliance as the offering commences. Receipt of an I-924 exemplar approval is also a marketing advantage, as it shows investors that USCIS has approved the project from a compliance perspective, which eliminates the risk of a denial or delay related to any question about the project.

INVESTORS

Setting aside retrogression, the EB-5 program offers the fastest and most flexible way for overseas investors to immigrate to the United States. It's also the only permanent visa that offers a passive investment for immigration where an investor could, for example, invest in a project in Miami but reside in Los Angeles.

With investment as low as $500,000, plus a $50,000 administrative fee, legal, and other miscellaneous costs, the EB-5 program also provides a low-cost means of immigration, given the expectation of recovering the $500,000 investment in approximately five years. The law requires that every dollar of that $500,000 be spent on project costs, while the administrative fee is used to pay ineligible costs, such as commissions and regional center fees. Attorney and document fees add another

$20,000 to $30,000. After return of the investment, the true cost for an entire family to permanently immigrate to the US is approximately $80,000, thus making it far more affordable than any other immigration pathway.

Because EB-5 investments historically have not offered a meaningful financial yield (the green card has been positioned as the "return" on investment), investors focus on two primary objectives:

- Getting the permanent green card
- Return of their capital when projected

Accordingly, EB-5 investors focus on the traits of a highly marketable project noted in the prior chapter.

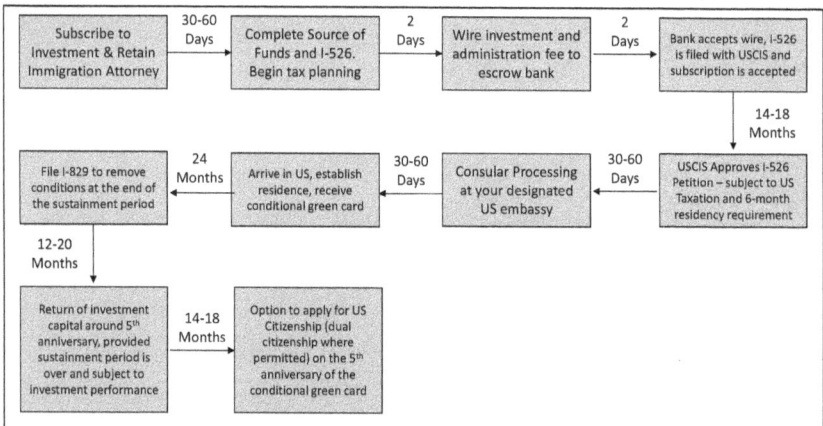

REGULATORS
USCIS

United States Citizenship and Immigration Services (USCIS) is a division of Homeland Security that administers and provides oversight of the EB-5 program. USCIS investigates and adjudicates all investor-applicants based upon a detailed review of the investor's SOF, completion of an extensive background check, as well as vetting the chosen EB-5 investment to ensure that it complies with EB-5 rules. Approved applicants receive a conditional green card, and USCIS also reviews the I-829 application to remove the conditions after the sustainment period. USCIS also grants regional center approval and, as of December 5, 2017, has approved 876 regional centers across the country.[41] USCIS staff conduct ongoing compliance monitoring and field audits of regional centers, New Commercial Enterprises, and Job Creating Entities. Most significantly, USCIS has broad authority to create regulations to carry out the legislative intent of EB-5 law and work cooperatively with other agencies, such as the FBI, SEC, and Department of Justice.

FINRA and the SEC

The Financial Industry Regulatory Authority (FINRA) is

---

41 "Immigrant Investor Regional Centers," U.S. Citizenship and Immigration Services, last updated October 1, 2018, https://www.uscis.gov/working-united-states/permanent- workers/ employment-based-immigration-fifth-preference-eb-5/immigrant-investor- regional-centers.

a self-regulatory organization (SRO) that oversees securities firms in the United States, protecting investors by ensuring the securities industry operates fairly and transparently. The SEC is a government agency that enforces federal securities laws and also provides regulation for the securities industry. Together, FINRA and the SEC act as the regulatory body for broker-dealers, providing licensing and testing to ensure the integrity of US financial markets and accountability to the investing public.

FINRA must approve each investment product type offered by a broker-dealer, including EB-5 investments. Before authorizing the sale of any investment product, FINRA requires the broker-dealer to demonstrate that it has personnel with the requisite experience and written supervisory procedures that ensure the compliant offering of the product to the investing public, including foreign investors. FINRA maintains a website for investors to research the background of broker-dealers and their registered representatives (https://brokercheck.finra.org/). Also of importance to investors is the ability to file a complaint with FINRA about an investment product purchased through a broker-dealer, to ensure access to fair and efficient dispute resolution.

Broker-Dealers

Generally, broker-dealers operate independently from

regional centers, development projects, and New Commercial Enterprises, which enables them to search the market for projects they feel are most suitable to meet the needs of EB-5 investors. Broker-dealers have an obligation to carry out extensive due diligence before offering any EB-5 investment. Broker-dealers must be able to critically evaluate the job creation potential and financial projections of any project so they can assess the potential for investors to achieve their objectives of obtaining a permanent green card and return of capital.

In addition to job creation and financial due diligence, broker-dealers also conduct extensive background checks on the developer, regional center, and New Commercial Enterprise manager, as well as all other parties critical to the success of the project, like the general contractor and property manager. Broker-dealers also review real estate matters such as the construction budget, legal entitlements, and valuation of contributed assets. While broker-dealers aren't responsible for preventing fraud or the failure of a project, their diligence and oversight during the capital raise and funding process significantly reduce the risks.

After performing due diligence, broker-dealers work with the New Commercial Enterprise issuer to market the offering both abroad and domestically, something that can only be done by a broker-dealer or officers of a New

Commercial Enterprise under the issuer's exemption. In order to fulfill their duties, broker-dealers must acquire basic knowledge of the investor to ensure they only offer suitable investments. In order to assess suitability, broker-dealers must obtain information from investors about their objectives, risk tolerance, net worth, liquidity, and prior experience before presenting any investment product, including an EB-5 investment. Because broker-dealers are regulated and accountable to FINRA and the SEC, the use of a broker-dealer to market an EB-5 investment bolsters confidence from investors, since they work with an independent party that owes them a duty of suitability and they have a path of recourse through FINRA arbitration should any disputes arise.

Regional Centers

A regional center is a construct of the EB-5 program that is not part of permanent legislation. Created in 1993, regional centers serve as a mechanism to facilitate the grouping of passive EB-5 investors into a larger project.[42] Investments through regional centers are permitted to count indirect and induced jobs as part of the job creation requirement, which enables larger EB-5 capital raises.

---

42 Annie Anjung Lin, "Splitting the EB-5 Program: A Proposal for Employment-Based Immigration Reform to Better Target Immigrant Entrepreneurs and Investors," Chapman Law Review, Vol. 18:2, (February 16, 2015): 538–529, http://www.chapmanlawreview.com/wp-content/uploads/2014/09/Lin.pdf.

Regional centers have due diligence and USCIS compliance obligations. The formation of a regional center typically costs over $100,000 and takes around eighteen months to gain approval, so forming a regional center does not make sense for one-time or smaller projects. Broadly speaking, ownership of regional centers typically falls into one of three categories: municipally sponsored, developer sponsored, and private non-developer sponsored. Many municipalities have formed regional centers as an economic development tool to provide developers access to EB-5 financing without forming their own regional center. Municipally sponsored regional centers often operate as "rent-a-centers" that do not assist in the capital raising process, recovering their operational costs through modest fees on each project.

Developers who plan multiple projects over a longer period of time in a local economic area, or projects of significant scale, can justify the time and cost to form their own regional center. This provides peace of mind, since the developer maintains control of all projects within their regional center and they do not have to worry about collateral damage if an unrelated project falters.

Non-developer private parties also operate regional centers. These regional centers operate as full-service entities, typically providing EB-5 financing while also conducting due diligence, providing term sheets, raising capital, and managing the mezzanine loan to the project. They are usually independent from the project, which benefits investors seeking separation between the EB-5 lender and borrower. However, these groups offer little value to developers if they lack a reliable source of EB-5 investors or access to bridge funding for the project to proceed while the EB-5 capital is being sourced.

Traditionally, real estate construction projects in gateway cities have been in high demand, which has led to concerns about unequal access to EB-5 in other parts of the country. Congress and regional centers from non-gateway cities are trying to level the playing field by motivating EB-5 investors to fund projects in rural areas and the so-called flyover states. Prior attempts to incentivize investors through draft legislation include changing how a TEA is defined using "priority rural" and "priority urban" definitions, which would eliminate most gateway city projects from the lower investment threshold.

Other levers to influence the choice of investors include the difference in the amount of investment required in a priority versus nonpriority area and setting aside a limited number of priority visas annually that would not be subject to the retrogression wait line. Attempts at long-term legislative renewal of the regional center program are widely expected to include these or similar provisions to enhance the accessibility of EB-5 nationally. What's more, they are expected to apply retroactively, as drafted in the failed legislation of March 2018.

As discussed in the next chapter, failed attempts at a long-term solution reside principally within the industry, as these changes are, not surprisingly, being resisted by the regional centers in gateway cities that are enjoying great success raising EB-5 financing.

CHAPTER FOUR

LEGISLATIVE INTENT

Like the old expression "Beauty is in the eye of the beholder," EB-5 stakeholders have their own views on the legislative intent of the program, which shapes their view of potential changes to the program to achieve long-term renewal of the regional center program. Broadly speaking, proposed changes to the program address the following:

- The legislative intent of the program
- Accessibility of EB-5 financing
- Increasing the investment amount to keep pace with inflation
- Integrity measures to protect investors

Core to legislative intent is the creation of jobs with an incentive for investors to invest in a TEA with an investment amount of $500,000 instead of $1 million. However, there is no uniformity between states when designating a TEA, which creates unintended consequences.

For example, critics point out that the State of New York will certify a TEA created for a project located in lower Manhattan by connecting it through a trail of contiguous census tracts to the Bronx, encapsulating all of the high-unemployment census tracts in the South Bronx. Supporters point out that employees come from areas like the South Bronx. In contrast, the State of California only allows a maximum of twelve clustered contiguous census tracts. Stakeholders debate about whether or not the New York policy is "gerrymandering," lacking credible connectivity to show job creation within a reasonable commuting distance to areas with high unemployment. Some feel that the legislative intent should be incentivizing projects located within high-unemployment census tracts, while others believe it is chiefly to employ persons commuting from high-unemployment census tracts. Whatever the case, draft legislation has proposed that USCIS adjudicate TEA designations to apply a uniform standard across all states.

Centralizing and revising the definition of a TEA is a contentious subject among industry stakeholders, with competing objectives lobbying for different standards. Not surprisingly, regional centers and developers in gateway cities that benefit the most under the current system oppose changes that would make a TEA designation harder to obtain. At the other end of the spectrum, regional centers and developers in non-gateway areas support tough restrictions that would create a level playing field because they struggle to compete with high-profile projects in globally known cities. More stringent standards to obtain TEA status would give investors an incentive to invest in non-gateway areas. The conflict between large regional centers in gateway cities such as Los Angeles and New York and regional centers located in smaller cities and rural areas has left the industry fragmented, with two competing factions that are bitterly opposed to each other in terms of how to balance future regulations.

A group of legislators led by Senator Chuck Grassley of Iowa, Representative Bob Goodlatte of Virginia, and Senator Patrick Leahy of Vermont propose carving out visas from the annual allotment specifically for rural and "urban priority" developments. Urban priority would have a fairly narrow definition, using distress criteria from the successful New Markets Tax Credits program to target single census tracts that have high levels of poverty (greater than 30 percent), low levels of income (less than 60 percent of the area median), and high levels of unemployment (more than 1.5 times the national average). Of the 10,000 visas available annually, their proposal would set aside 1,500 visas for rural areas and another 1,500 for priority urban projects that would allow investors from retrogressed countries to "jump the line" as an incentive to invest in these projects that are largely overlooked today when compared to those in gateway cities.

Other legislative proposals to level the playing field include priority visas and reduced investment amount incentives for manufacturing and infrastructure projects due to the economic ripple effect that these investments have on the economy. Manufacturing investments create quality jobs and fulfill a political goal to bring manufacturing back to America. Infrastructure in the US is aging and falling behind the rest of the world, creating a clear need for investment in this sector. The average age of airports in America is around forty years,[43] bridges are falling apart,[44] and rail transit lags behind much of the rest of the world.

Legislative changes will most likely impact the amount of the investment, which has not changed since the inception of the program. As we've mentioned, current investment levels stand at $500,000 for a TEA project and $1 million for a non-TEA project. All of the proposed

---

43   Tracey Lindeman, "Want to Fix American Airports? Build a Better Train Network," Motherboard, January 11, 2018, https://motherboard.vice.com/en_us/article/mbp554/want-to-fix-american-airports- build-a-better-train-network.

44   Conor Ferguson, "More than 50,000 American Bridges Are Falling Apart," NBC News, January 29, 2018, https://www.nbcnews.com/news/us-news/more-50-000-american- bridges-are-falling-apart-n842356.

bills adjust investments in TEAs to a minimum level of $800,000 up to $925,000, and those in non-TEAs from $1 million up to $1.2 million.[45] However, due to the inactive nature of Congress, USCIS circulated their own draft regulations that would raise the investment threshold to $1.35 million in a TEA and $1.8 million outside of a TEA.

Increasing it to $1.35 million raises the cost of an investment in a TEA project by 170 percent. Many investors simply can't afford the program at that rate and won't participate, but the increase also means developers will have to source fewer investors to raise the same amount of money. Therefore, they won't need to create as many jobs. It's possible that the number of investors will shrink proportionately to the increase, but if not, it may actually expand the amount of capital available. Fewer investors also means more unused visas to apply toward retrogression. Even with the increase, EB-5 is still a bargain compared to investment programs in other countries. For example, developers in Cyprus are selling property to Chinese investors at $2 million or more. Ultimately, Chinese agents have told us that the increase in proposed legislation is fine, as long as retrogression gets fixed.

The wide variety of proposed changes represent numer-

---

45   Jeanne Calderon, EB-5 Program: It's Broken, When Will It Be Fixed? NYU Center for Real Estate Research, April 5, 2018, http://ilw.com/immigrationdaily/news/EB-5-BrokenProgram452018.pdf, p. 16.

ous competing interests, any of which could potentially create significant hurdles for developers should they come to pass. However, all parties generally agree on the need to ensure the integrity of the program and the need for increased compliance. In fact, the last three versions of draft legislation featured virtually identical integrity and compliance measures. In the next two chapters, we'll take a look at the implications of the proposed "integrity measures" and the draft rules of compliance that will likely be imposed by new legislation.

CHAPTER FIVE

INTEGRITY MEASURES

The current EB-5 market differs significantly from the market a few years ago. Not that long ago, prominent regional centers maintained that they were not marketing "securities," but instead were marketing an "immigration program." That mentality, combined with little oversight from regulators, enabled several high-profile fraud cases, which put the program under a bright spotlight.

Since 2013, six draft bills to legislate long-term renewal of the regional center program have been circulated and all have had nearly identical comprehensive integrity measures.[46] Each bill differs in the approach to address TEAs, investment thresholds, and other criteria that impact the

---

46 Bill Comparison Chart, "Comparison of S. 1501, H.R. 616, H.R. 3370, S. 2122, S. 2115, & SKILLS Act," EB-5 Investment Coalition, accessed June 20, 2018, http://eb5coalition.org/resources/bill-comparison-chart/.

marketability of EB-5, but all share a common thread: EB-5 participants would have to become compliant with all US securities laws and subject to higher levels of accountability, compliance, and audit requirements. Accountability would increase dramatically for regional centers, project sponsors, and any party affiliated with an EB-5 transaction. Currently, many regional centers rent their status to third parties, surrendering all responsibility for the inner workings of projects. However, under the proposed integrity measures, regional centers would become fully accountable to certify compliance.

The consistent inclusion of integrity measures in draft bills suggests that any long-term legislation will make it far more difficult to execute an EB-5 transaction without broker-dealer supervision. Broker-dealers are fully acquainted with US securities laws and the rules of FINRA, have detailed supervisory procedures to follow those rules closely, and will play a vital role in the transition to greater compliance and the institutionalization of EB-5.

BRINGING EB-5 INTO THE FINANCIAL MAINSTREAM

The regulations by which broker-dealers operate derive from the Securities Act of 1933 and the Investment Company Act of 1940. The Securities Act of 1933 came about as a direct result of the stock market crash in 1929 as a means of creating more transparency in financial statements so investors could make informed decisions. It established regulations for the offer and sale of securities in an attempt to curb fraud. Prior to this, such regulations were left in the hands of state governments.

The Investment Company Act of 1940 spelled out the kinds of activities an investment company can get involved in and provided standards for the entire industry. As a result, the US financial services industry has become tightly structured, highly regulated, and consequently highly reliable. Anything related to capital, both in the public and private sector, now has a structured system behind it. When broker-dealers first stepped into the EB-5 marketplace, they brought those systems and regulations with them, albeit with much resistance from entrenched industry stakeholders.

Before broker-dealers started getting involved in the EB-5 program, migration agents and regional centers functioned as the conduits for transactions. These roles have evolved over the years. Early on, salesmanship dominated, and the motto of agents seemed to be "Just keep talking until the deal is closed." However, after a few failed projects and fraud cases, agents learned the value of professional diligence and got serious about becoming a financial intermediary to protect their reputation and business. Today, while still employing aggressive sales tactics, reputable agents from larger firms conduct their own due diligence. Their income depends on it.

Unfortunately, migration agents still lack accountability from a US regulatory authority to operate with the transparency of a broker-dealer. Fees and conflicts of interest are carefully hidden from investors by agents. There is no compliance oversight because the government considers them merely immigration consultants. The government perceives the agent's role as a connecting service between would-be immigrants and applicable programs in the US. While shaping up their due diligence, agents are sometimes willing to stretch truths, omit details, and use pressure tactics to close sales, which creates risk for project sponsors and regional centers, which must certify compliance with all securities laws under the proposed integrity measures.

Migration agents act as investment professionals to foreign investors who are otherwise left to search the internet for an EB-5 project, unable to adequately perform due diligence on their own. Without a broker-dealer, or any regulated intermediary, investors are at the mercy of the migration agent, with no guaranty that they can trust the agent's word.

Weak EB-5 projects are often marketed with gimmicks and window-dressing intended to take advantage of cultural differences and distract investors from flaws in the business model or investment structure. For example, a hotel revenue bond, falsely marketed as safe, might be structured so that the standard 2 percent room tax is increased to 6 percent, with the city using the 4 percent increase to service the revenue bond. To a foreign investor, this may look safe on paper, especially as part of a persuasive sales pitch, because it implies that the bond is backed by the full faith and credit of the municipality. But what happens if there aren't enough room sales? Room sales below projections means there will not be enough taxes to service the bond, and the city won't impair its credit rating to back it. Since the city's involvement makes the structure look especially trustworthy, agents will allow investors to overlook the real risks of the investment.

With robust oversight and enforcement from FINRA and the SEC, broker-dealers have a meaningful deterrent to engage in the self-serving instincts of migration agents, which enhances investor confidence and raises the marketability of the investment. While the investment world offers no absolute guaranties, the presence of a broker-dealer engenders trust that a project has been thoroughly vetted at an institutional level, that fees are transparent, and that all conflicts of interest have been disclosed.

Broker-dealers straddle the line between fairness and

efficiency when working with a project to structure the investment, advocating for a structure and offering that will—in their judgment—be marketable, bring cost-efficient capital, and stand up to regulatory scrutiny, even if things do not go as planned.

THE FOX IN THE HENHOUSE

As we mentioned earlier, in most fraud cases, the party responsible for the management of the lending party (the EB-5 New Commercial Enterprise) was also affiliated with the project (Job Creating Entity). In other words, the fox was in the henhouse.

When a bank or institutional lending organization makes a loan, they secure the loan with documentation heavily in favor of the lender and their ability to preserve their capital. If the project falters and defaults, prudent lenders will aggressively exercise their default rights, including foreclosure. However, if the manager of the New Commercial Enterprise also has a vested interest in the project, there is a significant conflict of interest that may incent the manager to act in their own self-interest, which may not align with the interests of the EB-5 investors.

Despite this conflict, assuming both roles is not illegal, provided the relationship is disclosed in the offering materials—a lack of disclosure would constitute securities fraud. However, the disclosure is generally placed deep in the private placement memorandum and the investor is at risk to read and discern the conflict on their own. Broker-dealers require independence between the manager for the New Commercial Enterprise and Job Creating Entity to avoid this material conflict altogether.

In the wake of retrogression for investors from China, Vietnam, and India, the role of an independent manager has become even more critical to manage the investors' funds should redeployment become necessary to maintain the "at risk" requirement for EB-5 investors during their sustainment period. Most projects that raised capital before 2016 didn't have provisions contemplating redeployment. Managers for those projects are now, or will soon be, dealing with how to manage through redeployment.

New Commercial Enterprises managed by a party related to the project developer may be tempted to use the proceeds to fund additional party-related developments using the broad authority granted in most New Commercial Enterprise operating agreements. However, if that authority and the potential for investor funds to end up in another project was not disclosed as a risk factor in the PPM, the manager could potentially be exposed to a claim of securities fraud by an investor.

New Commercial Enterprises managed by an independent party will take a more conservative approach when managing redeployment in situations where it was not contemplated in the original offering. Working with immigration counsel, an independent manager will seek suitable alternatives that maintain the "at risk" requirement and minimize the financial risk, since the investor will have satisfied the job creation requirement at that point in time. The investor does not have a financial upside under the structure, so a fiduciary will seek to minimize the financial risk to match the limited financial return. As an additional step to avoid a claim of securities fraud, a best practice is to offer several suitable options to the investor—including a return of capital and abandonment of their immigration petition, since investors may want an exit, given the length of retrogression—and allow them to choose how their capital is redeployed.

Whoever manages the New Commercial Enterprise should have a vested interest in the investors' success and exercise a fiduciary duty to look out for their best interests. This separation is another growing pain in an industry evolving toward institutional practices that will lead to better accountability, protection for investors, and a reduction in risk for developers and regional centers.

CASE STUDY: THE JAY PEAK RESORT CASE

The Jay Peak Resort in Vermont drew negative attention to the EB-5 program. Though it became one of the most widely reported fraud cases in the history of the EB-5 program, it did not begin with ill intent. Early projects from these Vermont developers were legitimate and on pace with the rest of the region: slow, steady, and quiet. Initially, everything proceeded aboveboard, but along the way, the developers became aware of a greater potential for capital, and their priority shifted. Rapid access to capital is great when it supports a well-vetted project supported by a third-party market study, but problems arise when sourcing capital becomes the first priority and responsible deployment becomes an afterthought.

The state-sponsored regional center lacked sophisticated diligence and disbursement processes, creating an opportunity for the developers to commit fraud once the amount of funds raised exceeded legitimate uses. Governor Peter Shumlin and Senator Patrick Leahy participated in trips to find investors and raise funds, and because the regional center was creating jobs and raising money, the momentum encouraged the developers to think bigger and continually add more. Fundraising happened without proper internal controls.

Within a few years, Vermont's EB-5 developers accrued millions of dollars, but none of the oversight systems adjusted to match the volume. Adding a broker-dealer to the mix might have provided the set of independent eyes the Jay Peak project needed to make sure transactions were structured, marketed, and executed with integrity. Instead, money was accessed and used without oversight, with some funds sloughed off for apartments in New York, some for airplanes—whatever the developers could think of. More than $50 million wound up being used for fraudulent purposes. Each successive project covered the gaps in the previous one, so it became a Ponzi scheme operating in an unregulated EB-5 marketplace.

When the deal finally fell apart, investors lost their money and found their immigration statuses at risk. The bankruptcy attorney who became the receiver for the case lacked experience in EB-5 but quickly learned that the investors consisted of two distinct stakeholders: investors who had already obtained their permanent residency and wanted their capital back, and investors who simply wanted access to a green card.

To examine the Jay Peak case, the federal receiver, Michael Goldberg, needed an expert on the job creation side of the EB-5 program. Without a legitimate economic model for counting the number of jobs created, some of the investors would have lost the opportunity to obtain a green card.

Tom Martin, part of Baker Tilly's EB-5 consulting team, worked directly on the Jay Peak case after the fraud was uncovered. He helped structure a resolution to best protect the immigration benefits of the investors. Fortunately, the receiver, along with immigration counsel, Ronald Klasko, were motivated to this end. The ensuing investigation tracked all the way back to the origin of the project to determine if any job-creating activities had been missed on the front end that affected the end result, and indeed, over 2,500 additional jobs were claimed to preserve the green cards of over 250 unsuspecting investors. Ultimately, former Jay Peak owner Ariel Quiros was ordered to pay back $80 million to investors, was fined $1 million by the SEC, settled a fraud case with the State of Vermont for $2 million, and was ordered to pay $2,515,798 of prejudgment interest. However, an accountable third party or broker-dealer likely would have prevented this fraud from occurring in the first place.

WEEDING OUT MARGINAL PROJECTS

In an ideal world, everyone involved in EB-5 would have a vested interest in robust compliance, but a number of industry participants continue trying to shortcut the system. For that reason, Congress has discussed bringing a fairly heavy hand to enforce compliance measures that are consistent with other US financial markets. By exposing industry participants to a potential claim of securities fraud, which will pierce corporate structures used to limited personal liability, the attraction to think short-term about projects and other compliance requirements will wane.

Broker-dealers are obligated by FINRA rules to offer only suitable investments to their clients, which places two burdens on the broker-dealer. First, the broker-dealer must perform due diligence on each investment before offering it to prospective investors. Chiefly, they examine two aspects of an EB-5 investment that align with the primary objectives of EB-5 investors: the credibility of job creation projections and the financial feasibility of the project in returning investors' capital. Second, in order to present a suitable investment to a client, the broker-dealer must learn the risk tolerance, investment objectives, experience, need for liquidity, source of income, and other relevant factors about the investor to ensure the investment is suitable to meet their needs in light of their preferences.

To assess job creation claims, diligence will focus on a review of the economic analysis, specifically the qualifications of the consultant preparing the report, the methodology and econometric model used, and the assumptions used by the economist to reach their conclusions. The broker-dealer will ensure that the methodology used is consistent with those accepted by USCIS and the reasonableness of the assumptions. To assess the financial feasibility of the project, diligence will focus on the source and use of funds, operational assumptions, and the exit strategy to return investors' capital. Due diligence by the broker-dealer is discussed in greater depth later in this chapter.

Through a professionally skeptical mindset, broker-dealers identify hidden deal killers by peeling back the layers of a project and investment structure to locate potential flaws in the project or management, abuse, or fraud, weeding out marginal projects. They also examine projects to answer the question, "Why is EB-5 money the right kind of capital for them?" If a project can be funded domestically for the right price, that's almost always the right solution.

In the Chicago convention center hotel case, the developer, Anshoo Sethi, produced promotional materials, claiming he had the backing of then-governor of Illinois Pat Quinn. In one brochure that he circulated in China, Sethi claimed to have fifteen years of experience as a developer when, in fact, he had no experience at all with major real estate developments. He also claimed he had franchise agreements with established hotel brands and that he had secured investments from the city of Chicago. He recently received a three-year prison sentence for fraud.

Because of the apparent endorsements, no one looked closely at the project. Minimal due diligence would have raised red flags. Last-minute complaints alerted the SEC to problems and caused them to freeze the escrow account before it was misappropriated. Money was ultimately returned to investors, but other cases have not ended so well.[47]

INSTITUTIONAL DISBURSEMENT OF FUNDS

Banks do not simply hand out money and send people on their way, yet that is exactly what many EB-5 projects have done over the years. A lack of institutional process in administering funds has been a common factor in cases of fraud. Fund administration should be a two-step process:

1. Receipt of investor funds into escrow
2. Disbursement of funds to pay for project costs (or as otherwise prescribed in the private placement memorandum)

There is no need for the developer to handle funds in either step.

In response to increasingly longer processing times for

---

47 Jason Meisner, "Developer Given 3 Years in Prison for Failed Convention Center Near O'Hare," Chicago Tribune, February 21, 2017, http://www.chicagotribune.com/news/local/breaking/ct-ohare-convention-center-fraud- met-20170221-story.html.

I-526 petitions, the industry has moved from the conservative practice of holding investor funds in escrow until approval of each investor's I-526 to virtually no use of an escrow account. Today, projects have access to investor funds as soon as they clear the bank's KYC and AML checks through its BSA department. In return, the sponsor offers investors a guaranty to return their funds in the event of an I-526 denial.

While this sounds good on its face, two questions arise:

- Does the sponsor have the liquidity to honor this guaranty?
- Is the sponsor required to make a best effort to replace the investors' funds?

If the denial is related to the project and not the investor, then the investor has lost valuable time and has to replace the investment. To limit exposure to the risk of project eligibility, investors should seek projects that have an I-526 exemplar.

In the event of an I-526 denial, the investor should read the I-526 denial documents very carefully because most of them are not blanket denials. If the project is raising $40 million, the denial might say the sponsor has to set aside $4 million—10 percent—to repay any investors who get denied. To honor this, the project will have to create a holdback, but if more investors get denied than can be covered by the holdback, they might not get their money back. If a project sponsor raises $50 million with the promise of covering the entire amount, it is unclear where the $50 million will come from to guarantee the I-526.

While developers comply with draw procedures imposed by commercial banks for traditional senior loans, the EB-5 industry has not afforded the same level of care to investor funds upon release from escrow. Best practices would dictate the use of a controlled disbursement account after investor funds are released. The process would be the same used by banks in that the developer submits a draw request, and an independent New Commercial Enterprise manager assesses the draw by inspecting actual progress and invoices, releasing funds after completing diligence to a title company for payment to subcontractors and collecting lien waivers. At no point should the developer need to have direct access to the funds.

Escrow and controlled disbursement accounts offer the best way to minimize compliance and investor risk. Adopting institutional fund administration processes is another milestone in the institutionalization of EB-5.

IF THINGS GO WRONG

Thorough due diligence, even if performed by a broker-dealer, does not guarantee success or that all flaws will be identified. In fact, in order to be eligible for EB-5, investor capital cannot be guaranteed, since USCIS requires the investment to be "at risk" through the completion of the sustainment period (filing of the I-829).

However, a good broker-dealer will independently monitor the project throughout the investment period, keep investors informed, and recommend action steps should any problems arise. With the involvement of a broker-dealer, the chance of fraud is significantly reduced, but any person who commits fraudulent actions can be held accountable through the court system. Project failure due to business risks such as an economic downturn or unforeseen market forces driving a project out of business falls within the definition of "at risk" investment, in which case there will likely be no recourse to any party.

Investors who fail to achieve their objectives of immigration and return of capital will likely want to sue someone. When a project fails and investors suffer a loss of capital, chances are good that investors will not recover damages from the developer. However, investing through a broker-dealer may offer an avenue for potential recovery through FINRA arbitration if the investor can prove a failure in due diligence, material misstatement, or omission in the offering materials.

Of course, not all broker-dealers are the same. Small "introducing broker-dealers" have a small minimum capital requirement of only $5,000 and may not have sufficient liability insurance to cover more than a few claims. Fly-by-night broker-dealers might simply disappear. They have no reputation to uphold and no global brand name to preserve. Investors seeking to benefit from working with a broker-dealer should make sure they are working with an institutional quality broker-dealer.

US MARKETS AND FOREIGN FINDERS

By law, only licensed broker-dealers can earn and pay commissions for selling securities within the US. However, Regulation S allows the issuer of a security, such as the manager of a New Commercial Enterprise, to market EB-5 securities overseas and pay a commission to foreign finders. These finders act as unlicensed broker-dealers and frequently engage in questionable selling practices and high-pressure sales tactics to earn substantial fees, as they are not regulated and held to the standards of transparency and integrity of US broker-dealers.

Because foreign finders are outside of the jurisdiction of the SEC, USCIS is attempting to compel regional centers, project sponsors, and other transaction participants to certify that all sales comply with US securities laws and all compensation is fully disclosed. The compliance requirements in some draft legislation have gone as far as requiring the naming of all foreign finders, along with how much they're getting paid. Some requirements have even demanded that they register with USCIS.

INFORMED AND SUITABLE

Broker-dealers are obligated to present only suitable investments to prospective investors, which means they need to assess and understand the investor's investment objectives, experience, risk tolerance, and financial condition. Broker-dealers collect this information through a customer account form. In the case of an EB-5 investment, the investor's objective should always be to obtain permanent US residency for themselves and their family and to preserve capital. Because EB-5 investments typically offer no appreciation and only a token financial return, the broker-dealer will ensure that the investor understands that EB-5 investments aren't suitable if their expectation is to achieve substantial earnings or to pay for educational expenses or retirement.

Assuming the objectives align with EB-5, the broker-dealer will assess risk tolerance. EB-5 transactions are sold as private placements and, as such, have no secondary market. In fact, private placements are generally restricted from being resold and are therefore illiquid. Most EB-5 investments involve the construction of commercial real estate, which is essentially a startup enterprise with no prior operational history. The project may not be fully leased or presold. No matter how experienced or financially strong the sponsor, this type of investment is clearly riskier than a US Treasury bill, municipal bond, mutual fund, or blue-chip stock. It is a moderately aggressive or aggressive investment, and investors should have their eyes open to that fact.

Because of the risks involved, a broker-dealer will assess the financial condition of the investor as a final step to determine suitability. Does the investor have sufficient income and other liquid assets to hold an illiquid EB-5 investment? Could the investor sustain a total loss? The broker-dealer can only conclude suitability through a transparent and fully disclosed process. In contrast, unlicensed agents and finders tend to gloss over the risks and tell investors what they want to hear. Remember, if it sounds too good to be true, then it probably is not true.

A transaction led by a broker-dealer will close with a fully informed investor making an investment that is suitable in light of their objectives, risk tolerance, and financial condition. While bad things can happen, the investor can take comfort knowing that an investment through a broker-dealer has helped them make an informed decision and take a calculated risk, hedged as much as possible by thorough due diligence that only an independent broker-dealer provides.

CHAPTER SIX

THE IMPORTANCE OF DUE DILIGENCE

Broker-dealers are required by their very nature to perform due diligence on an investment product before offering it to prospective investors. Under previously proposed EB-5 renewal bills (and expected integrity measures), regional centers would also be held accountable for performing due diligence. Thorough due diligence is a best practice to protect investors and regional centers from engaging in projects that might be subject to fraud or weak financial or operational fundamentals that could give rise to legal liability and reputational damage.

Each investment is unique, and diligence needs to be customized to fit the specifics of each case. However, due diligence can be broken down into several broad components, which bear similarity to many of the enhanced marketability features listed in Chapter 3, including the following:

- The structure and offering documents
- The development team
- Financial feasibility
- Real estate matters
- Job creation

STRUCTURE AND OFFERING DOCUMENTS

The structure of an EB-5 investment sometimes resembles a web of entities, and every entity has to be verified on a granular level. An organizational chart creates a visual flow chart to simplify the relationship and role of each entity involved in the transaction.

Dissecting the structure requires one to understand how funds flow from one entity to the next and the conditions required to transfer those funds. During this process, risks that might prevent the flow of funds can be identified, and conflicts of interest will become apparent based on the party or parties authorized to move funds through the structure.

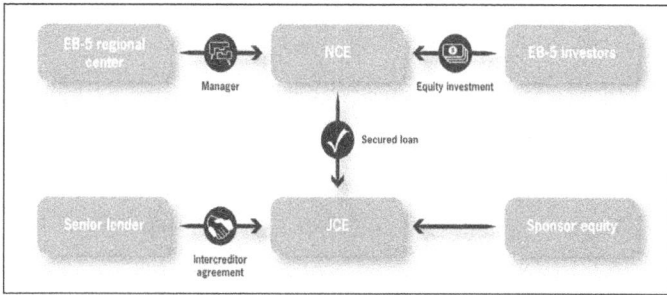

Typically, EB-5 funds are structured as a loan to the project. Careful attention needs to be given to the note, loan agreement, intercreditor agreement with the senior lender, and any collateral documents to ensure the terms are accurately described in the offering materials and are commercially reasonable to protect the interests of the investors as a lender. A popular technique used by EB-5 developers has been to have the New Commercial Enterprise make a "secured" loan to an intermediary entity that uses the loan proceeds to make a preferred equity investment in the Job Creating Entity, pledging the preferred equity as collateral to the New Commercial Enterprise to secure the loan.

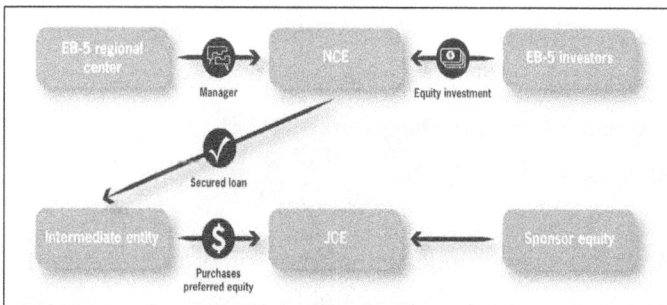

Immigration agents liberally marketed such investments as "secured," but in reality, after cutting through the semantics of the structure, they are typically unsecured preferred equity investments. If the project has a bridge loan, those terms should be reviewed for full and accurate disclosure, especially if there are any conversion rights or punitive terms if the bridge loan is not fully taken out at maturity. Once the structure, risks, and conflicts of interest are fully understood, a final step is to review the offering documents to ensure full and transparent disclosure.

A broker-dealer or regional center may find certain conflicts of interest too risky to accept, such as having the manager of the New Commercial Enterprise related to or affiliated with the Job Creating Entity. However, it is important to remember, as mentioned earlier, that conflicts of interest are not prohibited, provided they are fully disclosed. While full disclosure may protect from a claim of securities fraud, disclosure does not relieve the New Commercial Enterprise manager from their fiduciary duty to look out for the best interests of the investors. However, the existence of the conflict introduces risk that the related party manager may not act as aggressively as an independent manager.

A broker-dealer will also pay particular attention to the use of an escrow agent and the conditions for releasing the investor's funds to the project. Due to long processing times by USCIS, the market has evolved to use a hold-back or I-526 denial guaranty structure, but given the low denial rate of I-526 petitions (the fourth quarter of the 2017 fiscal year saw an I-526 approval rate of 93 percent),[48] a holdback of 10 to 20 percent of investor funds will generally create a pool of liquid funds to return capital to any investor who is denied after all appeals are exhausted. Under the denial guaranty structure, a responsible party guarantees the investor a return of their capital in the event of a denial. Good due diligence includes verification that the guarantor has sufficient net worth and liquidity to honor the guaranty. Finally, a comprehensive review of the offering documents, including exhibits, should ensure that there are no material misstatements or omissions that would give rise to a claim of securities fraud.

The private placement memorandum describes the plan to market the offering, which must comply with US securities laws. Every offering of securities in the US must be registered with the SEC, unless it qualifies for an exemption from registration. The two exemptions from registration available to EB-5 offerings are under Regulations D and S.

Regulation D is the exemption traditionally associated

---

48 Megan Stewart, "USCIS FY2017 Q4 I-526 & I-829 Statistics," First Pathway Partners, December 18, 2017, http://www.firstpathway.com/blog/uscis-fy2017-q4-i-526-i-829- statistics.

with the private placement of securities in the US. Under Rule 506(b) of Regulation D, privately placed securities may be offered and sold in a nonpublic manner to accredited investors, and up to thirty-five nonaccredited investors. An accredited investor is a person with a net worth (excluding home equity) of $1 million or more, or a person with an annual income of $200,000 or more in each of the last two years with the reasonable expectation of maintaining that level of income ($300,000 if measured jointly with a spouse). Rule 506(b) also permits the issuer to self-certify their accredited status.

Rule 506(c) permits the public solicitation of the unregistered security, provided it is sold only to accredited investors, and the issuer is obligated to collect documentation from the investor to reasonably verify that the investor is accredited. Whether sold under rule 506(b) or (c), because Regulation D sales occur within the US, transaction-based compensation may only be paid to a licensed securities broker-dealer.

Regulation S is the most commonly used exemption for EB-5 investments. Under Regulation S, the offer and sale of US securities may be conducted offshore to foreign persons using general solicitation, such as seminars and advertising, and without regard to the accredited status of the investor. Under Regulation S, fees may be paid to finders who are non-US persons.

	Reg D Rule 506-b	Reg D Rule 506-c	Reg. S
Pros	• May rely on investor to self-certify accredited status • Can be used for offers within the US • Allows up to 35 non-accredited investors (but this increases compliance costs)	• Permits general solicitation (television, radio, newspapers, social media, seminars, etc.) • Can solicit investors within the US	• Must be conducted in an "Offshore Transaction" • No limit on non-accredited investors • General solicitation permitted overseas
Cons	• Does not permit "general solicitation" (including: social media, public seminars, etc.) • Cannot safely be used with Reg. S outside the US, if using general solicitation marketing techniques	• Does not allow any non-accredited investors • Investor's accredited status must be verified with credible documentation (cannot rely on investor self-certifying)	• Documents must be executed offshore • No directed selling efforts (including general solicitation) in the US • Not recognized by California as a state level exemption from registration

Another exemption that often creates confusion is the "issuer's exemption." The issuer's exemption is not an exemption from registration, but it does exempt employees and officers of the issuer from the requirement to register as brokers in order to participate in the solicitation and sale of a private placement. While exempt from registering as a broker, an officer or employee of the issuer may not receive transaction-based compensation, such as commissions, whether sold under Regulation D or S.

BACKGROUND CHECKS

Conducting due diligence on the management team requires more than a Google search. Best practices start with a visit to the project site and sponsor's office to ensure everything exists as it has been presented. The project site should be owned, under option, or under lease by the developer. Entitlements, zoning, and municipal approvals should be in hand or well underway.

Next, the project management team's experience and background must be checked. Use of a professional background agency ensures that sponsors do not have a criminal history, bad credit check, undisclosed prior bankruptcy, or undisclosed project failures in their history. Open and concluded lawsuits should be reviewed as well to assess the reasons for the suits and to assess the character of management.

Third parties key to the success of the project need to be assessed. Does the general contractor have a track record of building projects of a similar scope and scale? Are they bonded? If there is a third-party manager/operator, do they have the experience and current capacity to take on this project? If there is a leasing or sales agent, do they have the expertise to successfully market the space? Which law firms have been engaged as security and immigration counsel? What is their experience and track record?

Is anyone else providing money to the project? If, for example, the brochure states that 20 percent of the money comes from tax credits, are those New Markets Tax Credits? Even if someone wrote a letter of intent to give money through a certain funding source, that letter of intent is nonbinding. When was the letter written? Five years ago? Yesterday? Has anyone contacted the company that wrote the letter to make sure it's real?

Are there equity investors in the project who aren't involved in development? If so, they might be purely financially driven. Where is the cash equity coming from? Is every source legal? In the Chicago convention center case, no one contacted the franchise companies to verify an agreement was in place, and one of the franchises turned out to be a fake agreement.

Ultimately, it should be verified that competent professionals structured the project.

REGIONAL CENTER DILIGENCE

Ownership and management of regional centers generally fall into four categories. First, some are captive to developers that plan to develop extensively within the geographic region for an extended period of time. Rather than pay a third-party regional center, they have chosen to invest in creating their own source of investors and manage compliance risk. Generally, developer-controlled regional centers stick to funding their own projects rather than taking a risk that a third-party project might cause reputational harm to their regional center. However, developer-controlled regional centers tend to lack any third-party oversight and are most vulnerable to fraud.

A second category of regional centers operate as financing companies, with the source of capital funded by foreign investors instead of shareholders and depositors. These regional centers tend to operate professionally and treat investors with a high degree of care, as their reputation and business model are dependent upon investor satisfaction. These regional centers perform due diligence, structure the transaction, issue a term sheet, raise the funds, and perform asset management and loan servicing during the life of the EB-5 loan.

Third, municipalities form regional centers as an economic development incentive to give developers low-cost access to the benefits of associating with a regional center without having to form one or associate with a for-profit regional center. While inexpensive to use, these regional centers tend to be characterized by a lack of due diligence or provision of other services—fundraising in particular—to projects. The projects have to determine their own structure, create their own offering documents, and source investors. Similar to developer-controlled regional center projects, there is usually no third-party oversight afforded to protect investors.

Fourth, a number of regional centers are formed to generate fee income from developers who need quick access to an existing regional center or in instances where it does not make economic sense to form a dedicated regional center. These regional centers create the most risk for developers and investors since they generally lack "skin in the game." They might be incented to take lower quality projects, while skimping on diligence and disbursement procedures. If the regional center folds due to problems, it can taint an otherwise good project and may impair pending I-526 applications for investors.

When selecting a regional center, project sponsors should not only conduct diligence on the owners and management, but the other projects already associated with the regional center. Even if all existing projects are progressing with no problems, a troubled or failed project during the marketing period will damage the marketability of a new project, even if it is independent of the troubled project. A final step is verification of the regional center's good standing with USCIS.

FINANCIAL ANALYSIS

Financial analysis covers the life cycle of the project, including the construction budget, operational assumptions (or history, if applicable), and exit strategy to return investors' capital. Generally, EB-5 investments fund new construction, and the budget needs to be reviewed. Diligence should assess if the budget sufficiently covers construction for the proposed project. After getting comfortable that the project can be built with the proposed budget, other sources of funds (equity, debt, and any incentives) should be verified as committed and not contingent.

Typically, land may be purchased from a related party or contributed as equity by the developer. The most conservative approach credits the value at the lower end of cost or current market value, but in all cases the value should be supported by a recent appraisal from a qualified independent appraiser. Finally, best practices include a completion guaranty from the developer, and the ability of the developer to fund change orders and cost overruns.

If the project is to be built with a guaranteed maximum price (GMP) contract, diligence needs to extend to the financial capacity of the general contractor and an assessment of the construction documents. Investors can get a false sense of confidence when they hear the developer has a GMP contract. GMP contracts stipulate that the price is based on the level of detail in the construction documents, with allowances for costs not yet fully known. The developer can adjust the price of the GMP contract upon finalizing those costs.

After completion of construction-phase financial diligence, projections must be assessed. Are revenue assumptions supported by an independent market study from a credible expert? Is there any preleasing? If so, do the assumptions for space to be leased seem reasonable in light of the terms in the executed lease? Are there any presales? If so, what are the terms? Can buyers easily walk away from the presales, or do they have a substantial, nonrefundable deposit? Are hotel occupancy and rate assumptions consistent with their competitive set? Has the operational manager reviewed and approved the projections? Similarly, expense assumptions should be put through considerable rigor to assess if the project can reasonably achieve the expectations outlined in the projections.

For an operating business or expansion project with historical financial statements, three years of audited financial history should be reviewed to ensure that the forward-looking projections are reasonable for both revenue and expenses.

If projections appear reasonable, then the cash flow must be checked to ensure the project provides a likely exit potential for investors and that the timing reasonably coincides with the expected completion of the immigration process (filing of the I-829 form).

Exit strategies typically fall into two categories:

- Sale of the asset (e.g., condos)
- Refinancing

Third-party market studies will provide insightful information about the supply of competing products, trends in the velocity of sales, likely selling prices, and concessions. Projects relying on a refinance (e.g., hotel, office, retail, or residential rentals) need to achieve an appraised value and demonstrate sufficient cash flow to cover the proposed level of debt needed to refinance the EB-5 investors.

A typical analysis estimates the value of the project using the projected cash flow at the time of the refinance with a capitalization rate specific to the property type and market. Depending on the type of property, banks typically loan 60 to 80 percent of the appraised value, provided the cash flow can support a debt service coverage ratio of 1.2 times or greater.

Highly specialized financial due diligence is required based on the type of property being financed, including third-party reports to assess if the projections can reasonably be realized. A developer can make any project look good with an Excel spreadsheet, but a skilled diligence expert will sift through the assumptions to separate institutional-quality projects from weak projects.

REAL ESTATE DILIGENCE

Real estate diligence starts with verifying the legal existence and good standing of the entities involved in the transaction, ensuring that the land is held by the Job Creating Entity or under contract to be purchased at closing. Environmental diligence follows, and a Phase I report will indicate if conditions exist that warrant soil testing. The file should conclude with documentation to support no contamination, completed remediation, or an approved plan if remediation is within the scope of the project.

An independent appraisal should be obtained from a qualified appraiser that reports three values: "as is," "as completed," and "as stabilized." The "as is" value should support the value of contributed equity if shown as an SOF. Additionally, a report of title should be obtained to ensure all taxes are paid, with no undisclosed liens against the real estate. Finally, evidence of insurance and all approvals, permits, and zoning should be reviewed and verified to ensure that the project is "shovel ready."

Last, critical contracts should be reviewed for commercially reasonable terms and disclosure of any related party matters. Major contracts include those with the architect, general contractor, franchisor, and property manager.

JOB CREATION ANALYSIS

Achievement of the immigration benefit, the green card, depends upon providing evidence that ten US jobs were created per investor. However, when it comes to assessing the risk associated with job creation, all jobs are not equal.

In addition to counting model-driven direct jobs, projects associated with a regional center are allowed to calculate and count indirect and induced jobs. Projects not using a regional center may only count full-time employees. Direct jobs are those that can be observed and counted on a payroll report. The downside to direct jobs is that they are subject to a good economy and successful operation of the project. One of the first costs cut after disappointing results are direct jobs. Operational performance and general economic conditions can have a negative impact on the number of direct jobs created for purposes of achieving a green card.

Indirect jobs provide goods and services to the project but aren't directly employed by the project. Construction jobs create both direct and indirect jobs, but you can only count the direct construction jobs when the project goes past the two-year mark. Prior to that, they are counted as indirect jobs, and in some instances, they are considered induced jobs.

Construction jobs are calculated by an economist using a

computer model (e.g., IMPLAN or RIMS II) that utilizes inputs such as the cost of construction, location, time to build the project, and the percentage of hard-cost materials and furniture, fixtures, and equipment used that are produced within the US. On average, construction usually costs more than budgeted and takes longer than expected, so there is usually very little risk associated with the creation of construction jobs. The main risk associated with the creation of construction jobs is ensuring that the project is fully funded and that the project is actually built. The risk of funds and completion can be mitigated with the use of a bridge loan and completion guaranty.

Induced jobs are created by direct or indirect employees of the project as they spend their paychecks in the local community. Induced jobs are calculated by an economist using a computer model that utilizes economic inputs. Like direct jobs, if the project does not meet projections, the inputs that drive the econometric model will project a lower level of job creation.

Diligence procedures for job creation include reviewing the report and credentials of the independent economist, such as their track record of USCIS approval on prior economic analysis reports comparing the methodology used with those accepted by USCIS and a review of the assumptions used in the econometric model to ensure they are transparent and supported by third-party data.

Additional comfort can be gained by hiring another economist to prepare a report to compare results for reasonableness. Generally, a broker-dealer will size an EB-5 offering to ensure a cushion of at least 30 percent excess jobs over the minimum requirement.

TARGETED EMPLOYMENT AREA

Since EB-5 investments have historically not offered an opportunity for commensurate financial returns, investors prefer to invest the lower amount of capital enabled through a TEA. Under the current law, TEAs are certified through a state agency. Also, while marketing the investment, investors must invest with a TEA designation that is less than one year old. Therefore, capital raises that extend twelve months beyond the date of the initial TEA certification need to have the TEA renewed. Investors who submit their I-526 with a current TEA are protected from a future change in the designation.

Given the recent proposals to change TEA designations, project sponsors would be wise to show cautiousness in going to market with a complex TEA that may lose its status should the law change in a manner consistent with prior draft legislation.

....

CHAPTER SEVEN

....

REGIONAL CENTER COMPLIANCE

For many years, EB-5 investments went largely unnoticed by regulators. USCIS regulated program participants, and since USCIS focused its diligence toward investor applicants, compliance with securities laws was not on the radar. With little or no coordination or communication between USCIS and the SEC, the EB-5 industry largely operated without a strong understanding of how to comply with securities laws.

A number of regional centers rationalized that an EB-5 investment did not meet the definition of a security. Due to this lack of understanding, an environment persisted that was vulnerable to fraud, and often participants didn't fully understand that they were paying illegal commissions. If not for complaints to the SEC by investors, this may never have come to light.

Now, compliance and integrity measures are fixtures in all draft legislation, and responsible stakeholders clamor for the industry to adopt the best practices of institutional financial markets.

INTEGRITY MEASURES

As we've discussed, the current EB-5 market differs significantly from the market a few years ago. With China in severe retrogression, competition for investors has intensified to a whole new level.

Fraud in EB-5 put the program under a harsh spotlight, making it clear that securities and stricter regional center compliance is required. Several senators have circulated draft bills to promote integrity measures. While each bill differs on how to modify the definition of a TEA and the minimum investment, all have shared nearly identical compliance language that would require EB-5 participants to certify compliance with all US securities laws.

Accountability requirements would increase dramatically, especially for regional centers that operate as "rent-a-centers."

Currently, many regional centers rent their status to third parties. Some of these "rent-a-centers" perform little or no due diligence, do not participate in structuring the offering, raising the capital, or performing any measurable services. They collect fees for allowing projects to attach to their status, claiming to save developers the time and money necessary to establish their own regional centers in order to count indirect and induced jobs for their EB-5 offering. However, under the proposed integrity measures, all regional centers would become fully accountable for diligence and would be required to certify compliance with the offer and sale of EB-5 securities, along with all other USCIS compliance requirements for regional centers.

Legislators have made it clear that any long-term renewal of the regional center program will include these integrity measures, making it far more difficult and riskier to execute an EB-5 transaction without the assistance of professionals. With the burden of certifying compliance falling on all transaction participants, even those who were previously passive, risk-averse developers and regional centers should consider passing the compliance risk to a broker-dealer since they are in the business of securities compliance.

PROPOSED COMPLIANCE LEGISLATION

Legislative changes on the horizon assign accountability

to EB-5 transaction participants. The Fraud Prevention and Detection proposal, for example, includes integrity measures and transparency requirements for regional centers, as well as requirements for robust disclosure to investors.

FEE DISCLOSURES

The substantial fees for placing EB-5 investments run higher than most US investment products, and foreign agents have not always clearly disclosed their fees to investors. Rather than an attempt to deceive, many foreign agents were simply unclear about the need to disclose the exact amount of all fees, but growing awareness of the need is changing the industry.

FINRA requires full transparency on fees, and investors are often required to sign a fee disclosure, similar to a Truth-in-Lending disclosure for a consumer loan or mortgage. The language describing the compensation in the PPM has drawn criticism in proposed legislation for not being fully transparent and clear.

ACCOUNTABILITY

The Fraud Prevention and Detection proposal focuses on regional center accountability, which in theory creates more accountability for everyone involved in an offering.

It bars non-US nationals from regional centers, as well as people with criminal violations that led to a year or more in prison, or anyone connected to civil judgments in excess of $1 million in the past ten years.

Though stalled, current draft bills assert that Homeland Security should conduct biometric background checks, photographs, signatures, and fingerprints of everyone directly involved or affiliated with the regional center, the New Commercial Enterprise, or the project (Job Creating Entity). Under this legislation, all parties would get checked before conducting the offering, and USCIS would conduct periodic field audits to ensure continued compliance.

It's possible that many regional centers and promoters will resist the magnitude of reforms, arguing that they are already subject to standard compliance under Regulation S. Currently, USCIS already does random site visits, but legislation could make it mandatory to visit every site at least once.

Legislators have also included language in the proposal that protects investors who fall into noncompliant situations by allowing them to move their investments to a new regional center and project without losing their priority date with USCIS. If current draft legislation ever moves forward, implementation in real practice should prove interesting.

CERTIFYING COMPLIANCE WITH SECURITIES LAWS

Historically, the EB-5 industry has primarily relied upon Regulation S to use foreign finders to source investors, though many regional centers were unaware of the questionable tactics used by some of those foreign finders.

As explained in Chapter 6, Regulation S provides an exemption from registering the securities offering with the SEC. In order to qualify for this exemption, all marketing, offers, and sales must occur offshore to non-US persons, which describes most potential EB-5 investors. This exemption provides numerous benefits: investors do not have to be accredited, the investment may be marketed using general solicitation techniques, and nonlicensed foreign finders may be paid a fee for referring investors. The main caveat to Regulation S is that no directed selling efforts may occur from within the US, though in practice, this nuance has yet to be tested by regulators. However, in the age of the internet, avoiding directed selling could prove difficult because of the open flow of information.

To hedge against this risk, most EB-5 offerings are conducted under a dual exemption that also includes Regulation D. Regulation D provides an exemption from registration with the SEC for private placements offered and sold within the US.

Securities marketed in the US are generally conducted by a FINRA broker-dealer; however, it is permissible for the officers of the issuer (New Commercial Enterprise) to market the investment directly without being a licensed broker under the "issuer exemption." While the issuer must ensure that each investor is sourced in compliance with Regulation S or D, the open flow of information on the internet, the use of dual registration exemptions, and the issuer exemption often leave issuers unclear about how to classify investors and could potentially lead to noncompliance.

Since this is difficult to detect by regulators due to their limited resources, all parties, especially those not directly involved in sourcing investors, should use a broker-dealer to supervise the offering and ensure robust compliance.

Certifying compliance with US securities laws also includes the payment of commissions, finder fees, or any other characterization for transaction-based compensation. Only licensed broker-dealers may accept transaction-based compensation for facilitating the sale of a security, whether or not the security is registered or exempt under Regulation S or D. Even under the issuer exemption, officers of the New Commercial Enterprise affecting the sale of an EB-5 investment may not be paid compensation that depends upon, or is related to, the outcome or size of the transaction.

Further adding complexity to the issue, a growing number of investors from India already live in the US under an H-1B or student visa, and it's unclear whether or not they are considered "US persons" in regard to which regulations they fall under.

In regard to foreign finders, there is no set definition in US securities laws. The "finder exemption" is a concept derived from the collective interpretation of numerous SEC no-action letters. In the general view of finders, they do nothing more than provide the contact information of a potential investor to an issuer. Finders should never participate in important parts of a securities transaction, including soliciting, negotiating, or execution.

Compensation to finders must be appropriate in light of their activity and not tied to the size of a transaction or its closing. Also, a finder should have no history of facilitating securities transactions or handling the funds of those making an investment. As a concept derived through the interpretation of prior SEC no-action letters, the "finder exemption" provides an opportunity for the SEC to refine its position on finder activities at any time.

This should give transaction participants reason for concern. The duties foreign immigration consultants have historically carried out are often at odds with the widely accepted practices of a foreign finder, as derived from SEC no-action letters, such as the following:

- Presenting the investment
- Answering questions about the investment
- Negotiating terms such as the final amount of the administrative fee
- Assisting with completion of the subscription agreement, investor questionnaire, and other required documents to facilitate the sale
- Receipt of significant fees contingent upon the closing of the investment sale

Further, the dominant activity of these finders is the facilitation of securities transactions. Foreign agents even refer to themselves as "immigration consultants" because it's illegal to broker an investment in China without a license.

While referral fee agreements between an agent and the New Commercial Enterprise likely forbid all of these practices, transaction sponsors have been unaware of these actions, or comfortable accepting the risk given that US regulators have no jurisdiction over foreign agents and, in the absence of a complaint, lack the resources to proactively investigate these practices.

Finally, the use of Regulation S to offer and sell EB-5

securities to non-US persons does not provide any relief under the antifraud provisions of US securities laws. Antifraud provisions encompass more than simply testing for "material misstatements or omissions" in the offering materials. Antifraud provisions also hold issuers accountable for how their securities are marketed, including any inaccurate, inflated, misleading, or deceptive written or oral representations made by finders.

Antifraud provisions also apply when allowing a finder to engage in some or all of the prohibited activities above that substantively render a person labeled as a "finder" to be an unlicensed broker. A successful claim brought under the antifraud provisions gives the investor a right of rescission, meaning they have a right to pierce the limited liability of corporate entities (including limited liability companies and limited partnerships), even layers of corporate entities, to claim a refund of their entire investment plus interest from the individuals responsible for the offering.

OUTLOOK ON ENFORCEMENT

The future of enforcement remains to be seen. FINRA, a self-regulatory organization (SRO), oversees broker-dealer compliance but has no jurisdiction over issuers of securities.

Broker-dealers who engage in a wide variety of investment products have a revocable license that allows them to earn a very good living, provided they follow the rules of compliance. The potential loss of a broker license creates a strong deterrent, so a well-capitalized broker-dealer will not cut corners when offering any investment product, let alone an EB-5 investment. A sense of self-preservation, combined with periodic compliance audits from FINRA, results in an industry culture rooted in compliance.

As the arm of the federal government responsible for enforcing securities laws and regulating financial markets, the SEC has a three-part mission:

- To protect investors
- To maintain fair, orderly, and efficient markets
- To facilitate capital formation

In light of the SEC's mission, robust proactive enforcement of EB-5 issuers remains unlikely without a complaint or legislative mandate. While an investor complaint will trigger an action, the SEC will likely limit their investigation to resolving the complaint, not expanding into a systematic examination of the industry and its practices. With respect to orderly and fair markets, EB-5 investors have invested over $20 billion in the US economy since

2008, with over $5 billion invested in 2017 alone,[49] which makes it a small part of the $19.42 trillion US economy. Without a legislative mandate, the SEC has little incentive to devote significant resources to assert robust compliance over a sliver of the US financial markets—a conclusion reached by industry participants long ago.

Proposed legislation designed to modify the practices of regional centers and other EB-5 transaction participants would result in robust compliance that resembles other financial markets, with the threat of severe consequences under the antifraud provisions of securities laws. Regional centers would be less likely to engage in risky projects and sponsors. Requiring more transparency, compliance, and accountability over regional centers will spark positive change in the industry, increasing investor protection, confidence, and the overall integrity of the EB-5 program.

OUTSOURCING

Outsourcing investor services can take many time-consuming or overly complicated tasks off the plates of investors and developers. As retrogression forces many developers to take a hiatus so they can devote themselves to other projects, it might be helpful to have outside help

---

49   "U.S. Immigration and Foreign Investors," American Action Forum, January 24, 2018, https://www.americanactionforum.org/research/u-s-immigration-foreign-investors/.

to deal with all of the servicing obligations on prior EB-5 projects that have been closed. Outsourcing also transfers some of the risk to another party. The key is to work with a service provider who has appropriate policies, procedures, and processes around everything they do.

CONCLUSION

WHERE IS EB-5 GOING?

Retrogression has effectively shut down the EB-5 market in China. Upon learning of the length of retrogression in a presentation by Charles Oppenheim in April of 2018, some Chinese investors who had invested within the last three to five years (and have children who will likely age out due to retrogression) began asking for their money back, abandoning their EB-5 petitions to immigrate elsewhere.

Within the bounds of the current law, USCIS has a fair amount of latitude to implement regulatory changes, as already demonstrated by their notice to standardize the definition of a TEA and change the minimum investment threshold. In a highly publicized lawsuit, a group of investors seeks to force USCIS to change the policy of counting each investor and family member toward the annual cap of 10,000 EB-5 green cards. Presently, each investor and their derivatives account for multiple green cards. By only counting the investor, an estimated additional two to three times the number of EB-5 green cards would be issued to satisfy current demand, which would at least begin to eradicate the retrogression backlog. In fact, a precedent already exists for adopting such a change, making the treatment of derivative applicants consistent with how they are treated under the H-1B program. Under H-1B, the spouse and children of an H-1B applicant do not count toward the annual limit of visas.

Legislation seems less likely to produce a solution. Thus far, attempts to get a bill to the Senate and House floors to renew the regional center program has failed. The bills that have been presented offered no relief for retrogression. The House Committee on Appropriations recently attempted to add language to a spending bill that would have eliminated the initial allocation of 7 percent of annual EB-5 visas per country, which would add multiple years to every country (besides China, which is already in retrogression).

Addressing retrogression through legislation is tantamount to immigration reform, and since any effort to reform immigration will be both comprehensive and controversial, it seems unlikely to occur anytime in the near future. EB-5, as a comparatively minor component of immigration, lacks gravitas in such a politically charged arena, so it is unlikely to accelerate any immigration reform.

In the current political climate, where H-1B is being curtailed, few people care about wealthy foreigners who want to invest money in the US in order to immigrate. This is unfortunate because, ultimately, EB-5 brings billions into the country in a way that is inexpensive to developers. Investors tend to be affluent and ambitious entrepreneurs and high-skill professionals filling important roles in the tech world. They contribute to the US economy, buy homes in our communities, and send their kids to our colleges.

Without regulatory or legislative assistance to put the largest, most mature EB-5 market back in business, what happens next? The size of EB-5 capital raises will continue to shrink, the industry will continue to deploy resources to develop new markets, and the industry will contract. With market dynamics restricting access to the robust infrastructure that supports access to the world's largest population of millionaires in China, the days of finding hundreds of investors within several months are over. The size of EB-5 raises will shrink, and they already are. According to information obtained from NES Finan-

cial, five years ago, the average size of an EB-5 capital
raise was $52 million, whereas today it is $25 million.[50]

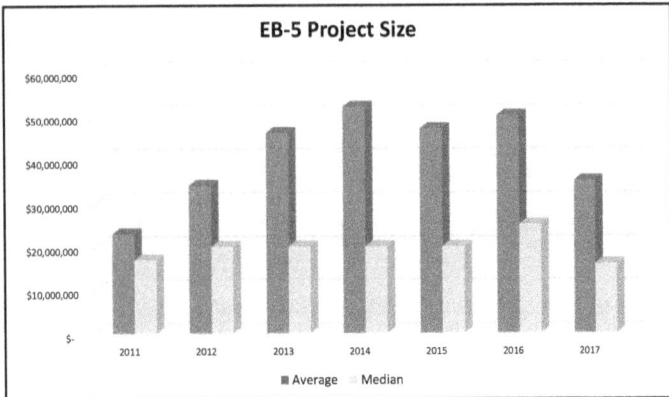

EB-5 Project Size

Source: NES Financial, used with permission

Emerging markets are immature and lack an infrastructure of immigration agents and a critical mass of
millionaires, so while EB-5 participation may be increasing in these countries, it is unlikely to return to the level
of investment seen in past years without participation
from the Chinese market. Additionally, Vietnam and
India recently entered retrogression, and the Brazilian
and South Korean markets will join them shortly. While
the heightened focus and resources spent on developing emerging markets improve access and efficiency to
raise EB-5 capital, these efforts simply cannot increase
the supply of qualified investors in those countries.

---

50   NES Financial, "Historical Trends in Project Size," International Law Weekend 2018, New
     York, New York, October 18–20, 2018.

If nothing else, the EB-5 industry has proven to be highly adaptive to market forces. As high-volume regional centers shift to new markets outside of China, they're entering brand-new territory, which is like starting over. As in the early days of EB-5 in China, it feels like the Wild West, where some people employ questionable tactics rather than best practices. Everyone has an opportunity to learn the lessons of the past, see the mistakes others have made, and try to do the right thing.

Sourcing investors in these new markets is a longer process, which begins with educating the market about the EB-5 program and marketing smaller capital raises in order to build a track record of closed projects. Networks of EB-5 investors in those countries, who endorse the program to their friends, family, and professional network, do not yet exist. The growth of EB-5 in a new market is not linear but geometric. As early adopters invest, word spreads to their sphere of influence, which triggers new investors, building momentum.

The inability to raise over $50 million in a reasonably short and predictable time frame may discourage large projects from using EB-5. Smaller, high-quality projects where EB-5 could be an attractive part of the capital stack may now have a unique opportunity, especially if the market or developer has connections to the foreign market. This may give rise to the industry taking projects to EB-5 markets that simply cannot qualify for or attract domestic sources of financing, which places those investors and the reputation of the program at risk. Many midsize developers and projects being pushed out by megadevelopers may now have a more level playing field when searching for capital.

Present market conditions encourage many participants to exit the market and focus their resources on greener pastures. As a result, the future of outsourcing asset and investor management responsibilities, especially in the face of increased compliance and integrity measures, is an emerging trend.

Natural forces in today's EB-5 market do not always incentivize participants to act in a manner that combines self-preservation and profit with investor safety and market integrity, which are necessary for the long-term sustainability of the EB-5 program. While the demise of EB-5 is not imminent, without a long-term legislated solution with regulatory oversight that alters current market forces to align industry behaviors with sustainable outcomes, EB-5 will continue to be pushed into more and more niche markets.

If that happens, EB-5 will fail in its laudable mission to attract foreign capital to fund development in areas of high unemployment, create jobs, and aid in the legal immigration of persons seeking to realize their dreams of US residency. The future of EB-5 may lie with smaller developers who use the capital for their own projects under a "friends and family" approach. However, if we finally see EB-5 reform with visa relief, the program could easily become a truly institutional form of capital.

ABOUT THE AUTHORS

KEVIN WRIGHT is an economist and consultant with the FINRA broker-dealer Baker Tilly Capital, and he previously founded Wright Johnson, one of the world's largest EB-5 consulting companies. The coauthor of The EB-5 Handbook, Kevin is a regular presenter at conferences and frequently travels to China, Korea, India, Mexico, Vietnam, Brazil, Turkey, the UAE, Russia, and other markets.

MICHAEL FITZPATRICK is a partner and board member with Baker Tilly Virchow Krause, LLP, the thirteenth largest CPA and consulting firm in the United States. In 2001, he co-led the formation of Baker Tilly Capital, where he leads its EB-5 practice and has closed more than $1 billion of specialized financing that includes EB-5, New Markets Tax Credits, and private equity. He is a regular panelist at conferences and has authored numerous articles on EB-5.

The authors contributed to this book in their personal capacities. The views expressed are their own and do not necessarily represent the views of Baker Tilly Capital, Baker Tilly Virchow Krause, LLP, or any other employer or organization.